Communication Among Health Professionals:

Improving Communication Through Education and Lifelong Learning

Iris Mercedes Berríos, PT, DPT, MPH, EdD

Communication Among Health Professionals:

Improving Communication Through Education and Lifelong Learning

Iris Mercedes Berríos, PT, DPT, MPH, EdD

Communication Among Health Professionals:
Improving Communication Through Education and Lifelong Learning

by
Iris Mercedes Berríos, PT, DPT, MPH, EdD

*A Textbook Presented in Partial Fulfillment
of the Requirements for the Degree of*

✳ DOCTOR OF EDUCATION ✳

UNIVERSITY OF ST. AUGUSTINE FOR HEALTH SCIENCES

Art by María Mercedes Gutiérrez Berríos

Ballast Books, LLC

www.ballastbooks.com
Copyright © 2025 by Iris Mercedes Berríos

ISBN: 978-1-966786-34-4

Printed in the United States of America

Published by Ballast Books

www.ballastbooks.com

For more information, bulk orders, appearances, or speaking requests, please email: info@ballastbooks.com.

Includes bibliographical references, index, and Appendix A.

This work is a textbook that was presented as a partial fulfillment of the requirements for the degree of doctor in education

Book cover: María Mercedes Gutiérrez Berríos

"Whether at our jobs or out in the world, communication with patients, family, friends, and strangers is an essential part of being alive. Effective communication can solve everything."

Communication Among Health Professionals:

Improving Communication Through Education and Lifelong Learning

Iris Mercedes Berríos, PT, DPT, MPH, EdD

CONTENTS

— AUGUST 2024 —

To the memory of my parents, Rafo and Iris, and my four grandparents, Carmen, Felo, Mercedes, and Jorge Guadalupe, a legacy of teachers who taught me the relevance of education. They inspired me to take the road toward discovery and happiness through the journey of lifelong learning. To my children, Iris, Jorge, and María, who keep me going, and to all my students, past, present, and future. Let's keep learning together!

Art by María Mercedes Gutiérrez Berríos

ACKNOWLEDGMENTS

I have been a physical therapist for more than thirty years. Since I come from a family of teachers, maybe it was my destiny to become an educator later in life. Their example nourished my love of learning, which later evolved into my passion for teaching. Becoming a formal educator has been my unreachable dream and an academic quest for many years. After finishing most of the courses as part of my doctor of education degree, I was going to start my dissertation process; one of my teachers thought that my investigation and experiences about communication should be shared through a textbook. She felt that I was capable of doing it. So, I pursued a different goal because I always believed in my professors and followed their advice. The final requirement to complete my degree as a doctor in education was submitting this book. I did it!

The days of research, thinking, analyzing, interviewing, and creating were endless. I often got tired and felt that the book was an unbearable endeavor. That being said, I want to thank all those who helped me through this past year and a half. First, my children, Iris, Jorge, and María, because they inspired me daily to keep going. Then, my family, friends, and colleagues. They believed in me and supported me. They were my champions all the way. We shared many coffees and ice creams and celebrated as I finished each chapter. Some helped with the technology and power failure issues. Others went with me to take breaks, going out for dinners, breakfasts, visits, vacations, and movies. Thank you, Vimaris, Menchu, Yomara, Monica, Mayrah, Robert, Rebecca, Lillian, Carmin, Waby, Edgar, Edith, Nelson, and my fellow EdD classmates Jacki, Melisa, and Samantha. My writing coaches, Dr. Adam Haley and Dr. Darcy Fox, thank you for your support and advice. Thanks to the people at Ballast Books, especially Lauren, Journey, and Emma, for the publishing process and making the book available to the world. This was a dream that came true. I will be thankful forever.

We transformed through learning together. Doing it surrounded by friends and family was both wonderful and challenging. I will miss this stage, but now I have new energy to follow other dreams.

CHAPTER ONE

Experiencing Communication Problems:
Learning Can Optimize the Process

Experiencing Communication Problems: Learning Can Optimize the Process

Communication is an essential skill for every health professional to fulfill the many complex duties of their work. Understanding, reflecting, and analyzing communication are vital processes to optimize it. Communication is when people send and receive precise and exact information that shapes and reforms behaviors, attitudes, and cognitions (Gephart & Cholette, 2012; Guttman et al., 2021). From our earliest moments, humans have relied on communication to navigate the world and accomplish essential tasks. To accomplish the best patient outcomes, the healthcare team must work cohesively as a unit (Carney et al., 2019; de Assis Brito et al., 2022; Nester, 2016; Pack et al., 2022; Ross et al., 2015; Royse et al., 2020). Correct, precise communication among team members is vital to achieving success (de Assis Brito et al., 2022; Gutmann et al., 2021). Communication is crucial throughout people's lives, especially when working as part of healthcare teams to ensure optimal patient outcomes.

The Consequences of Ineffective Communication

Ineffective communication costs hospitals an average of $2.2 million annually (Agarwal et al., 2010). When ineffective communication results in medication-related adverse events (MRAE), the costs vary significantly, depending on the area or country (Laatikainen et al., 2022). The estimated costs of medication-related adverse events in the United States varied significantly from $76.6 billion to $177.4 billion in research findings performed by investigators (Bates et al., 1997; Ernst & Grizzle, 2001; Johnson & Bootman, 1995).

From 2004 to 2006, Danish risk management research found that communication errors were reported as a significant factor in 70 percent of adverse events in health (Guttman et al., 2021; Rabøl, et al., 2011). Inadequate staff-to-staff communication and communication breakdowns continue to be the leading factors causing sentinel events in the United States (Joint Commission, 2023). A sentinel event is an incident that affects the patient's safety and is unrelated to the patient's illness, which causes harm (Joint Commission, 2023).

Communication mistakes need to be prevented to optimize our work and to increase productivity. Communication problems can affect the processes and the results of healthcare professionals' interventions, which directly affects patients (Guttman et al., 2021). Finding solutions to communication issues will improve documentation, ensure patient beneficence, reduce accreditation findings, avoid cost increases, and prevent costly remedial actions.

Structure of the Book

I (the author) wrote this book to immerse interprofessional health clinicians, professors, students, and everyone who feels the need to understand and improve their communication processes in an active and productive learning journey. Communication and teamwork are parts of health professionals' everyday lives. Effective communication will increase the odds of obtaining the best possible outcomes for every individual involved in the processes, especially the patients and their caregivers. This textbook will help the reader understand the many variables that can affect communication and how to improve the communication processes.

This textbook will provide effective tools to understand and solve healthcare communication problems. I encourage readers to consider their own communication experiences and to engage in an active learning process of reflection and analysis to improve team communication. This book will address different topics about communication, describing and analyzing real healthcare professionals' experiences obtained during interviews with nurses, physical therapists, physical therapist assistants, occupational therapists, occupational therapist assistants, speech language pathologists, nutritionists, social workers, and health administration personnel. In addition, this book will narrate my own personal experiences.

The topics covered in the chapters are: 1) The effects of ineffective communication and how health professionals need to work as part of effective teams; 2) Communication processes and styles, what affects communication, how to prevent communication mistakes, and how to optimize communication; 3) Communication barriers, its causes, and practical solutions; 4) Speak up, voice, and silence behaviors and communication tools to promote the speak up behavior; 5) Psychological safety and how to build trust in health professionals to increase their speak up behavior; 6) Power dynamics in the healthcare team and how to level the power to improve communication, 7) Attitudes and perceptions about communication and how to improve negative attitudes to promote communication in the healthcare team; 8) How to facilitate communication and create bonds among the healthcare team; 9) Healthcare learning and communication, including studies about the effects of ineffective communication in healthcare education and learning; and 9) How to improve communication skills in the healthcare team and in the classroom.

The Role of Learning About Communication to Improve Our Skills

Learning about communication will improve the reader's communication skills as they reflect, analyze, and understand. The investigation process and findings will be written using Kolb's Experiential Learning Theory (Kolb, 1984; McLeod, 2024a) and Maslow's Hierarchy of Needs (McLeod, 2024b). Maslow's Hierarchy will be used to analyze people's need for safety to promote their speak up behavior, which is using their words to speak out loud. The book will emphasize adult learners' needs and preferences from a practical perspective. The readers can start practicing what they learn through the book; activities and further readings will enhance the learning journey.

Kolb's Learning Styles and Experiential Learning

Kolb's Perspective applies a four-step cycle to the Interprofessional Competency Framework, which considers adult learners' characteristics and how they understand and apply their learning in practice (Kolb, 1984; McLeod, 2024a). Clinicians can describe the incident, reflect on the experience, learn from it, role-play, and experiment during similar situations in the future (Kolb, 1984; McLeod, 2024a). Students can go through cases and examples with their teachers, practicing the stages to get ready for their clinical internships.

Kolb understood that every person has their favorite learning style and that understanding it will facilitate the learning process (Kolb, 1984; McLeod, 2024a). Learning happens by feeling, watching, thinking, and doing, which are the basic actions described by Kolb's Learning Cycle. The cycle has four stages on a continuum where the learners prefer using a combination that can change depending on the situation (Kolb, 1984; McLeod, 2024a). The feel and watch stage is called the diverging stage (Kolb, 1984; McLeod, 2024a). During the assimilating stage, learners think and watch (Kolb, 1984; McLeod, 2024a). The converging stage is to think and do, and the accommodating stage is to feel and do (Kolb, 1984; McLeod, 2024a). See Figure 1 for a visual depiction of Kolb's Learning Cycle Stages.

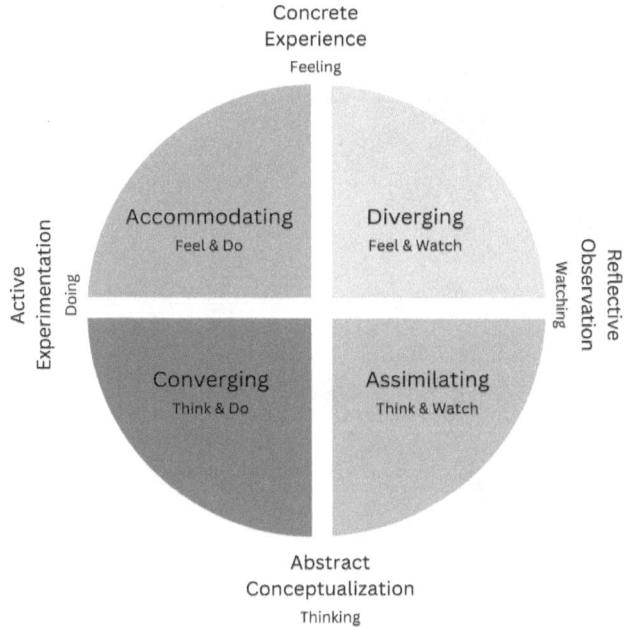

Figure 1 — Kolb's Four Stages of the Learning Cycle
Note: Graphic inspired by McLeod, S. (2024a, February 2).
Kolb's learning styles and experiential learning cycle.
Simply Psychology. https://www.simplypsychology.org/learning-kolb.html

The four-step cycle is easy to use, apply, and understand. Communication scenarios and experiences can be recalled, described, analyzed, learned, and practiced to improve team communication skills in the future. Adult learners can enjoy this experiential process while enhancing their understanding. It's learning by doing, remembering, analyzing, and experimenting with events to reach a significantly better understanding. From this process, learners get new knowledge and retain it longer in their memory, making it available for retrieval in the future. They can use and integrate their newly acquired knowledge into their daily lives to improve their communication skills and outcomes. See Figure 2 for a visual depiction of Kolb's Perspective.

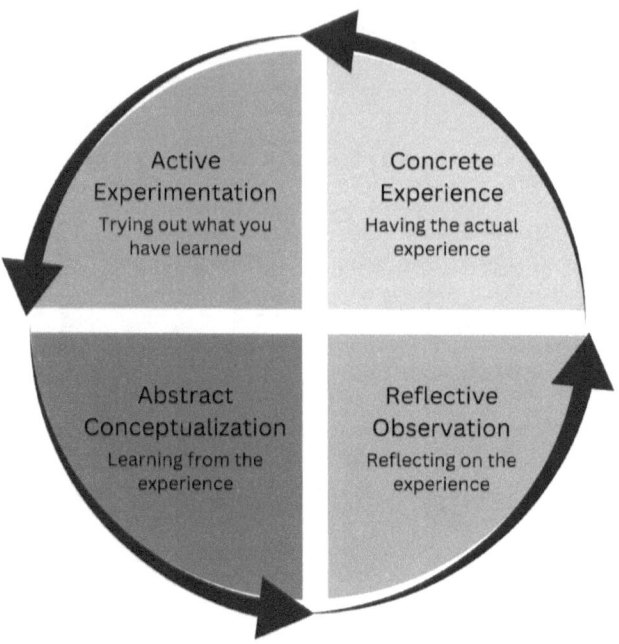

Figure 2 — Kolb's Learning Perspective Stages
Note: Inspired by McLeod, S. (2024a, February 2).
Kolb's learning styles and experiential learning cycle.
Simply Psychology. https://www.simplypsychology.org/learning-kolb.html

Kolb's Experiential Learning Theory provides four stages of the
Interprofessional Competency Framework (Kolb, 1984; McLeod, 2024a).
Cases will be worked using Kolb's perspective. The first step in the cycle
is the Concrete Experience (CE); the clinicians or students have their own
experiences with communication within their teams or with patients.
The second step is Reflective Observation (RO); they analyze and review
their communication experience situation and how it should have been
handled. The third step is Abstract Conceptualization (AC); they create
and answer Socratic questions to explore the experience, thus learning
and promoting better communication outcomes in the future (Kolb, 1984;
McLeod, 2024a). The questions used throughout the book will be: 1) What
happened? Describe the situation. 2) What went wrong? 3) List things that
should have gone differently. 4) What should be done next time? 5) How can
communication improve in a future experience? The fourth step is Active
Experimentation (AE); in this stage, role-play can be performed or discussed

to promote communication. Another way of doing this is by meeting once a month to discuss communication mistakes and review Kolb's stages in order to promote learning within the team. Throughout the book, the readers will discover communication elements and barriers and explore the meaning of psychological safety by analyzing communication patterns and reviewing past experiences, successes, and challenges. Immersing themselves in this learning experience will improve the reader's communication skills, helping them move forward toward self-development.

Maslow's Hierarchy of Needs

Maslow's theory describes human motivation and needs in a hierarchy (Maslow, 1943; Maslow, 1954; McLeod, 2024b). Maslow (1943, 1954) argued that the more basic needs must be met or partially met before higher needs can be addressed. The way in which you fulfill the needs is flexible depending on the individual and external circumstances (Maslow, 1943; Maslow, 1954). Each person will go through the levels in the hierarchy according to their experiences and environment. As a person's needs and motivations change and develop, Maslow's theory will help them understand themselves.

The first needs level is physiological: food, air, shelter, sleep, clothing, water, and reproduction (Maslow, 1943; Maslow, 1954; McLeod, 2024b). The next level is safety: personal security, employment, resources, money, and property. Love and belonging needs represent the next level of the hierarchy, which includes friendship, family, intimacy, and a sense of connection (Maslow, 1943; Maslow, 1954; McLeod, 2024b). Esteem includes respect, self-esteem, status, recognition, and freedom. The top level is Self-Actualization, which is the desire to reach one's highest potential in terms of creativity, morality, acceptance, and purpose (Maslow, 1943; Maslow, 1954; McLeod, 2024b).

To feel comfortable communicating and to communicate effectively, a person needs their physiological needs to be satisfied first. For example, if a person is hungry or has low blood sugar levels, the need to eat should be satisfied so that the individual can move on to higher levels. The second level of Maslow's Hierarchy is safety (Maslow, 1943; Maslow, 1954; McLeod, 2024b). Psychological safety is a perception of an environment

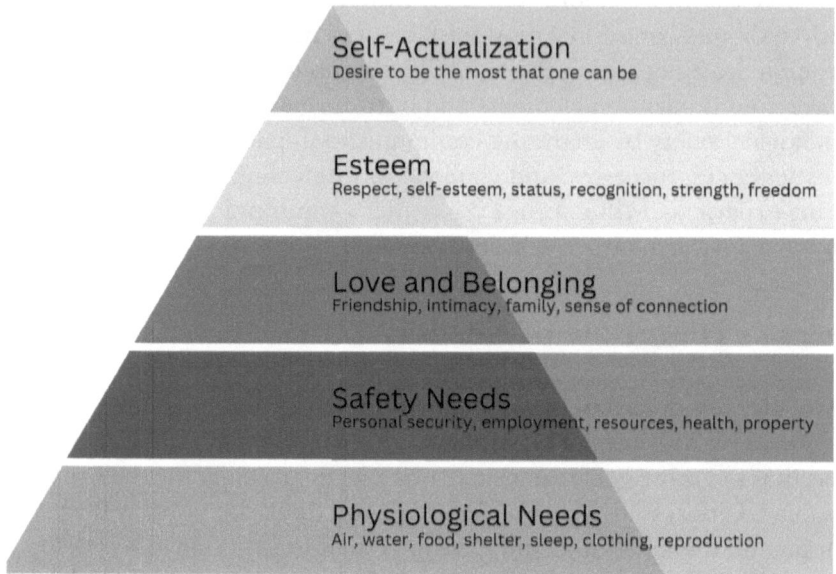

Figure 3 – Maslow's Hierarchy of Needs
Note. The image above was inspired by McLeod, S. (2024b, January 24).
Maslow's Hierarchy of Needs.
Simply Psychology. https://www.simplypsychology.org/maslow.html

where people feel safe to be themselves and express their views and experiences (Edmondson, 1999). When people feel safe, their motivation to use their speak up behavior increases. The feeling of safety will promote communication. Sometimes, clinicians do not speak up out of fear of being incorrect or perceived as incapable or incompetent (Guttman et al., 2021) or to avoid past negative experiences (Milliken & Morrison, 2003). Trust and safety must be felt among a healthcare team to facilitate the speak up behavior in the group.

For example, if a nurse feels that a superior is discriminating against her and interfering with her work, she should go to the clinical manager or human resources leader to talk about it to try to find a solution to the situation. If, on the other hand, the nurse feels that speaking up increases her risk of losing her job and brings her feelings of anxiety or fear, she will choose to remain silent. Silent behavior will not produce solutions to problems, and unless the nurse feels safe, she will not speak up. Chapter five will discuss how to increase psychological safety. Other levels of Maslow's Hierarchy can be associated with communication skills.

Communication skills can be related to love and belonging, the next level in Maslow's Hierarchy (Maslow, 1943; Maslow, 1954; McLeod, 2024b). Successful relationships need to be nurtured through communication. Communication is a good way to connect people because exchanging ideas and emotions is essential to building bonds such as friendship and romantic love. It is easy to understand how a lack of communication can interfere with human relationships. To develop stronger relationships, people need to share their feelings. When working with patients, good communication skills can enhance the patient-to-health professional relationship to forge a positive and productive human bond between them. This way, the health professional will be more invested in discovering and fulfilling the patient's needs. In addition, the patient will be engaged and ready to collaborate in their rehabilitation process because they've developed feelings of belonging as an active part of the health team. Analyzing how other levels of Maslow's Hierarchy relate to communication skills will increase the understanding of the relevance of speak up behavior.

Effective communication can be one of the paths to reaching people's esteem and self-respect, which are parts of the next stage in Maslow's Hierarchy (Maslow, 1943; Maslow, 1954; McLeod, 2024b). Using kind communication as feedback can teach the message's receptor about building positive experiences toward recognition and freedom. By the same token, communication can result in positive attitudes for the patients towards the health professional team. This will enhance teamwork and produce the best outcomes while patient collaborates with their own development to reach their goals.

The highest level of Maslow's Hierarchy is the desire to be the best person possible, which is the yearning for Self-Actualization (Maslow, 1943; Maslow, 1954; McLeod, 2024b). An important topic to discuss is how an individual needs to have the desire to improve their communication skills. The next step is to decide if they lack understanding or knowledge about communication to make improvements. For example, if the person feels that they communicate 100 percent effectively and others are to blame for their communication issues, they aren't taking accountability. They will not feel a need to develop their communication skills. It is important to reflect on how good communication skills can move people to higher levels of the hierarchy and bring people together to experience love, belonging, esteem, and self-actualization.

Reflective Points

- Have you been in situations where you felt that you could not speak up?
  - ⤻ Describe the situation and apply Kolb's Learning Perspective.
  - ⤻ Why did you prefer to remain silent?
  - ⤻ What were the specific reasons for your silence?

- What do you need to be able to use your voice?
  - ⤻ More time to reflect and plan what to say.
  - ⤻ Empathic and accepting peers.
  - ⤻ A relaxing environment.
  - ⤻ A welcoming leader who facilitates communication using cueing, prompts, and communication activities.
  - ⤻ To know your team members on another level through activities such as having lunch, going to the mall, or participating in communication workshops together.

Personal Experiences: Communication Problems

In the next section, real cases will be examined. The cases were drawn from my own experiences and interviews with colleagues. One of the reasons for writing the book is that many teammates inspired me to share our experiences to improve communication in other teams. They expressed excitement about the book because they experience communication problems daily, and it interferes with their work and services. They feel that they lose time and energy because of communication issues, making the book's topic relevant. Optimizing communication processes will improve our daily lives and our outcomes.

The process of reviewing real cases displaying communication issues in the healthcare field will bring to life the concepts studied, making the experience meaningful, interesting, and engaging. Examples of different communication issues will be narrated and discussed using Kolb's Experiential Learning Perspective (Kolb, 1984; McLeod, 2024a). Names were changed to respect privacy. Pay attention to each case so that you can perform your own reflection and analysis. The reader will learn vicariously through each relevant case, making it easy to recall each lesson and compare it to your own experiences.

Teresa's Case

⇒ Kolb's Learning Perspective Stages ⇐

1) **Concrete Experience**

   A physical therapist (PT) called a patient's home to schedule the start of care for the next day. When she arrived at the address she'd been given, she discovered it was not the patient's home. She called the home health agency's preadmission department to say that they'd made a mistake with the address, making her lose her time. She asked them in an abrasive way to recheck the information with other patients in the future so clinicians don't lose their time. She emphasized that this has happened frequently and that they should pay better attention to their work to prevent mistakes in the field. The preadmissions staff member explained that they would make their best effort to recheck patients' addresses in the future. She insisted that they are only human and that mistakes happened.

2) **Reflective Observation**

   Pre-admission personnel should have re-checked the patient's address through the telephone, repeating the address to the caregiver to verify correctness. Sometimes, masks and background noise can interfere with spoken communication. Abrasive communication should be addressed with the clinician physical therapist to promote a welcoming environment and improve teamwork.

3) **Abstract Conceptualization**

   a. What happened? Environmental and/or equipment noise and similar letter and number sounds may have interfered with spoken communication over the telephone during the preadmission process.

   b. What went wrong? The patient's address was not verified during the phone call. The incorrect address was sent to the PT. The PT did not verify the address during her call to schedule the visit with the patient's caregivers.

   c. What could they do next time to prevent miscommunication? Pay attention to the input of all those involved in the situation to optimize results in the future. Verify the information by repeating it to the other person involved in the communication process.

The PT should verify the address during the call to schedule the visit with the caregivers.

d. How to improve communication within the team? Communicate positively during the process. The supervisor should contact the PT to address her communication and its results to promote communication improvement and teamwork.

4) **Active Experimentation**
Discuss the case with the preadmissions department and clinical personnel to prevent the same situation.

Reflective Points

- Have you experienced a similar situation?
- Describe what happened and apply Kolb's Perspective.
- How have you prevented or solved communication errors in the past?
- What activities can be done to improve teamwork in your job?

Charles's Case

⚞ KOLB'S LEARNING PERSPECTIVE STAGES ⚟

1) **Concrete Experience**
A request was made over the phone by Charles's son to get a letter to explain to their paid caregiver's provider company what functional activities the caregivers were asked to do for the patient between physical therapy sessions to improve his condition. The physical therapist assistant's (PTA's) supervisor, Rose, got the call and called me to get my input about the patient since I was out after a fall. I told her to call the PTA who was doing the treatment sessions to assess the patient's status and, according to the case discussion, write the letter. Rose did not call the PTA for the status and wrote the letter only according to the occupational therapist's perspective. As a result, the letter was not updated according to what the patient needed from a PTA perspective. It only asked the caregiver to put the patient in bed for meals when what the patient really needed was to stand to improve balance. Rose showed me the letter, but I told her it had not been done according to the patient's status. She said that she had not had time to talk to the PTA and had done the best that she could under her circumstances.

2) **Reflective Observation**

The supervisor, Rose, should have called the PTA and gotten her data analysis to write a letter according to the patient's condition at the moment. Rose decided to create the letter according to her availability and standards.

3) **Abstract Conceptualization**

a. What happened? The letter was not written according to the patient's condition, which might affect the outcomes because the paid caregivers will only practice sitting and not other necessary activities.

b. What went wrong? Rose, the supervisor, did not have enough time to consult the PTA, so the letter was not as effective as it should have been.

c. What could they do next time? Pay attention to the input of all those involved in the situation to optimize results in the future. Maybe Rose should have spoken about her lack of time to me so I could offer my help with the letter when I came back from my sick days. In the future, she should manage her time more effectively in order to discuss the case with the PTA and plan what should be in the letter.

4) **Active Experimentation**

Discuss the case with the team to prevent the same situation.

Colleagues' Perspectives

During the creative process of the book, I (the author) performed interviews, and many colleagues decided to voluntarily bring their own examples and experiences to contribute to the learning experience. They expressed excitement about the book because they experience communication problems daily, and it interferes with their work and services. They feel that they lose time and energy because of communication issues, which is one of the reasons why this book is relevant.

During the interviews, some explained that when they use spoken communication, the messages are frequently lost or forgotten. Many prefer written messages using communication apps or email because there is written evidence later. Others expressed that some people don't communicate effectively and are closed to communication. They describe them as colleagues who prefer not to be bothered and worry about their own problems. Closed communicators are task-oriented and not interested in working as part of the health team. Negative attitudes such as aggressive, sharp tones and lack of respect for the team are the worst. These clinicians only worry about their own needs and interfere with the work of the rest of the team. Examples of their "victims" are auditors and assistants who require more detailed documentation, don't understand their handwriting, or require more information for incomplete progress notes. Closed or negative communicators are referred to in this book as "urchin communicators" because everyone around them tries to avoid communication with them to prevent being punctured by their abrasive communication practices. Whenever someone approaches the urchin communicator with a question or need for communication, they receive a "pinch" from them through their harsh responses. Eventually, people make their best effort to avoid every communication opportunity possible, even doing the urchin communicator's work for them to avoid talking.

Educational Activities

This section is an important part of the learning journey throughout the book. These activities and hands-on experiences will encourage reflection and foster a deeper learning process. Perform each activity carefully to optimize the effects on your communication skills. You can execute the learning activities individually, in pairs, or with your professional team. To facilitate the activities, a template was designed to be printed by the readers. It can be used as a visual-motor aid when working on communication examples. The template is included as Appendix A.

Role-Playing: Design Scenarios

a. Think about real-life communication problems that you've had. Recall the experience and take note of what happened. Create two examples, reflect on them, and discuss with a colleague what could have been done differently to improve communication in similar situations. Go back to Kolb's Experiential Learning Perspective to identify the process. Remember the experience, reflect on it, analyze it, and plan for future situations.

b. Recall past experiences of effective communication. Remember what happened and make notes. Create two examples, reflect on them, and discuss with a colleague what elements made the communication effective. Go back to Kolb's Experiential Learning Perspective. Recall the experience, reflect on it, analyze it, and plan for future conditions.

c. Recall, reflect on, explain, and analyze examples regarding the benefits of effective communication. What are the results of good communication practices?

Reflection Points

- Describe difficult situations that have happened because of communication errors.
- What do you expect from your colleagues regarding communication?
- Analyze if people understand you when you speak.
  - ⤙ How do people react when you speak up?
  - ⤙ Look for their nonverbal cues.
  - ⤙ Do they understand?
  - ⤙ Do you need to repeat yourself?
- Describe ways in which you can improve your communication.
- Are you an urchin communicator?
- Have you met an urchin communicator? Think about the experience.

As you read other chapters, you can come back to these examples to assess your learning process and see if you can solve the situations differently. In addition, you can recall and analyze other experiences from your past using the template in Appendix A. Practice will promote deeper understanding and improve your communication skills.

Further Reading

1) **McLeod, S.** (2024a, February 2). *Kolb's learning styles and experiential learning cycle.* Simply Psychology. https://www.simplypsychology.org/learning-kolb.html.
2) **McLeod, S.** (2024b, January 24). *Maslow's Hierarchy of Needs. Simply Psychology.* https://www.simplypsychology.org/maslow.html.
3) **Laatikainen, O., Sneck, S., & Turpeinen, M.** (2022). *Medication-related adverse events in Health care–what have we learned? A narrative overview of the current knowledge.* European Journal of Clinical Pharmacology, 1-12. https://doi.org/10.1007/s00228-021-03213-x.
4) **Agarwal, R., Sands, D. Z., Schneider, J. D., & Smaltz, D. H.** (2010). *Quantifying the economic impact of communication inefficiencies in US hospitals.* Journal of Healthcare Management, 55(4).
5) **Edmondson, A.** (1999). *Psychological safety and learning behavior in work teams.* Administrative Science Quarterly, 44(2), 350-383.

CHAPTER TWO

What Affects Communication

What Is Communication?

Communication is the key to opening the door to success for every health team. This book will explore and discover communication involving health professionals. Communication is the deliberate transmission of information or a message between people (Hobson et al., 2010; Sergy, 2017; Velentzas & Broni, 2014). Sergy (2017) described how communication is transmitted through diverse means:

- *Verbally* — using words through speech
- *Nonverbally* — using gestures, tone of voice, or other non-word indicators
- *Written* — blogs, books, letters, and emails
- *Visually* — visual art and aesthetic expression
- *Symbolically* — Morse code and shorthand
- *Chemically* — through secretions, pheromones, scents, and perfumes

The distinction between different forms of communication can be hazy, as with chemical and symbolic communication, which can be subsets of nonverbal communication, and sign language, which can be classified as a visual or unspoken verbal language (Sergy, 2017). Combining different communication channels is natural. Verbal and nonverbal language are usually blended (Sergy, 2017).

This book will focus on verbal communication, which is also called spoken or oral communication (Velentzas & Broni, 2014), among members of the healthcare team. Spoken communication includes interpersonal communication, such as discussions, speeches, phone calls, presentations, and face-to-face interactions. Tone and body language play an essential role in oral communication and can have a bigger influence on the listener than the actual information in the message (O'Reilly III, 1982). Spoken communication among the health professional team will be the main topic to explore during this learning journey.

Purpose of Communication

People must have a purpose to engage in communication (Hobson et al., 2010; Velentzas & Broni, 2014). Motivation is the first step to start the communication process; people involved need to feel the urge to send a message, speak up, create, or answer a message. The different purposes of communication are to tell, connect, discover, persuade, direct, amuse, and preserve (Hobson et al., 2010). Creating mutual understanding among participants, producing change, causing action, and sharing perspectives are other communication goals (Velentzas & Broni, 2014). Those who engage in the communication process, the sender, and the receiver, will need the drive, purpose, and motivation to respond; if they lack one or more of these factors, they will not respond, and communication will not happen.

For example, if the manager of a healthcare company wants to talk to a nurse about a complaint made by one of his patients and makes a phone call or email to communicate the information, the nurse may decide not to answer the manager's phone call or text message. Maybe another team member told him about the complaint, so he decided not to get the phone call. The communication will not happen because the nurse did not answer. The manager's purpose is to connect with the nurse to solve the issue and prevent future complaints. The purpose of the nurse is to avoid communication. Contradictory purposes will never promote an effective communication process.

Another example of breaking communication can be remaining silent during a meeting when a person asks a question, and no one answers. This behavior is common during face-to-face meetings or lectures. The purpose of the speaker is to promote participation, but the purpose of those who remain silent is not to communicate.

Effective Communication

Effective communication involves speaking and hearing; it happens when the message is accurate, not mistaken, and the result of the communication process is properly shared, interpreted, and acted upon between the people involved (Velentzas & Broni, 2014). The result of effective communication is that it accomplishes the purpose intended by those involved in the process (Velentzas & Broni, 2014). When communication fails to accomplish the purpose for which it was planned, barriers to the process should be analyzed to discover how the communication failed (Velentzas & Broni, 2014). The correct transmission of the message will produce, maintain, and potentiate the effect of the message. In the end, the purpose of effective communication is to carry the message, taking it to its fruition (Velentzas & Broni, 2014).

Modern medicine is very complex; the healthcare team must perform to its full potential to guarantee optimal patient care, and the teams must rely on effective communication patterns (Royse et al., 2020). Communication problems can affect the processes and the results of healthcare professionals' interventions, directly affecting patients (Guttman et al., 2021). The annual cost of ineffective communication in hospitals is an average of $2.2 million (Agarwal et al., 2010). When communication errors result in medication-related adverse events (MRAE), the costs vary significantly, depending on the area or country (Laatikainen et al., 2022). The estimated costs of medication-related adverse events in the United States varied from $76.6 billion to $177.4 billion in research findings performed by investigators (Bates et al., 1997; Ernst & Grizzle, 2001; Johnson & Bootman, 1995). Finding solutions to communication issues will optimize teamwork, ensure patient beneficence, increase productivity, reduce negative accreditation findings, avoid cost increases, and prevent costly remedial actions.

Components of Communication

There are diverse communication models. This book will utilize a simple communication approach. Communication happens through a system with three components (Sergy, 2017; Velentzas & Broni, 2014). The three components are 1) A way to release or send out the message, 2) A channel to get the message from one point to the other, and 3) A way to receive the message. (Sergy, 2017; Velentzas & Broni, 2014).

In home health settings, clinicians commonly use cell phones to speak. The message is emitted by the sender/initial communicator by talking. The words are transmitted through the channel of the cell phone, and the person receives the message by listening. Equally important, the person who sends the message must be able to encode the message, which is to transform the ideas into the message by using words. Then, the person who will receive the message must be able to interpret or understand the message (Sergy, 2017; Velentzas & Broni, 2014). Failure of one or more of the elements will mean that the communication process failed (Sergy, 2017; Velentzas & Broni, 2014). For a successful communication process, the three components are required. For further understanding of the communication components and the actions of the sender and receiver of a message, see Table 1.

One-Way and Two-Way Communication

Communication can be one-way, when the person receiving the message does not respond or reply, or two-way when those communicating respond and interact (Sergy, 2017). Examples of one-way communication are reading books, watching movies, listening to a song, or sending emails (Sergy, 2017). One-way communication route goes from the sender through a channel to the receiver; it has no response (Sergy, 2017). Two-way communication involves at least two people talking or interacting and starts when the receiver of the message responds, forming a loop, as shown in Figure 4 (Sergy, 2017) on following page.

Communication Components	The Actions of the Sender	The Actions of the Receiver
Way to release or send the message	Encodes; transforms ideas into words	Interprets; understands the words
Channel to get the message from one point to the other	Speaks using the channel, which works correctly. Examples: phone, video, voice message.	Receives or listens to the message using the channel, which works correctly. Examples: phone, video, voice message
Way to receive the message	Should know how to use the channel and send the message.	Should know how to use the channel and be open to receiving the message.

Table 1 — Communication Components: Sender and Receiver Actions

The left circle shows how effective two-way communication works; the right circle shows the communication cycle (Sergy, 2017).

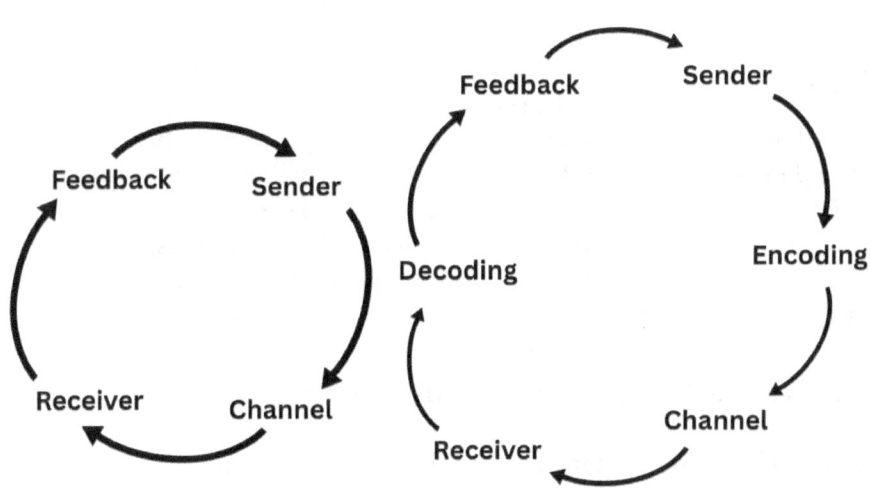

Figure 4 — Effective Two-Way Communication and the Communication Cycle
Note: Image inspired by: Sergy, L. (2017). What is communication? In Handy Answer: The Handy Communication Answer Book. Visible Ink Press. Retrieved September 18, 2023, from https://search.credoreference. com/es/articles/Qm9va0FydGljbGU6NDMyMzQyMg==

The communication cycle represents the elements of communication that follow a pattern (Sergy, 2017). See the right side of Figure 4 for a visual representation of the cycle. Understanding the communication cycle will clarify how communication is used. It can be used to plan a communication process, design a new communication method, and identify problems with its elements that may cause communication errors (Sergy, 2017). The elements of communication, as explained by Sergy (2017), are:

- **Sender** — the one who starts the communication.
- **Encoding** — making the words that form the message that will be communicated.
- **Channel** — takes the message from the sender to the receiver; it is a route or journey.
- **Receiver** — the one who takes or accepts the message.
- **Decoding** — the process of understanding the message; is executed by the receiver.
- **Feedback** — the response from the receiver; the answer to the message that the sender initially gave.

It is important to note that an issue or malfunction of an element of the communication cycle will result in communication mistakes. For example, suppose the channel does not work correctly. In that case, the communication will not travel effectively, as is what happens when the cell phone signal is too low and the sender and receiver of the message cannot hear each other. The words created by the message's sender should be clear and understandable otherwise, the receiver will not be able to decode or interpret the message correctly. Another example is if the sender and the receiver do not speak the same language or the sender uses technical words unknown to the receiver of the message. Equally relevant is that the message's sender can understand the feedback the receiver provides.

Skills Needed to Communicate Effectively

Several interpersonal and intrapersonal skills are necessary for communication; they include the ability to listen, observe, speak up, question, process, analyze, and evaluate (Velentzas & Broni, 2014). Those who receive the message should identify the speaker's purpose, take the content in, solve disagreements, interpret the information correctly, and decide how to respond to the message (Velentzas & Broni, 2014). These skills are the key to learning, creating relationships, and making a community to achieve success at work (Velentzas & Broni, 2014). These skills will facilitate communication and make it effective. Please see Table 2.

Skills Needed to Communicate Effectively	
Interpersonal Skills	Intrapersonal Skills
Listen	Process
Observe	Analyze
Speak Up	Evaluate
Question	Interpret Correctly
Take the Content In	Identify the Purpose of the Speaker
Solve Disagreements	Decision-Making — How to Respond

Table 2 — Skills Needed to Communicate Effectively

Communication Noises

As explained before, decoding or interpreting a message is an essential element of communication (Sergy, 2017; Velentzas & Broni, 2014). Communication noise involves the different influences that occur when people interpret or decode messages while talking to others (MacDonald, 2006). The words that compose the message are objective. However, each individual's interpretation is influenced by their experiences and environment. Communication noise can be overlooked but can have a significant impact on the receiver's interpretation of the message, perceptions of the sender, and communication analysis (Velentzas & Broni, 2014). This way, a message can be transformed by the receiver into something completely different from what the sender meant to transmit. The different forms of communication noise are psychological, physical, semantic, environmental, physiological impairment, syntactical, organizational, and cultural (Velentzas & Broni, 2014). Understanding communication noise is critical to identifying and analyzing communication successes and failures.

Psychological Noise

Psychological communication noise comes from the beliefs and assumptions of the individual, their biases about stereotypes, race, and reputation (Piaget, 1953). When a person gets into a conversation and has preconceived ideas about the other person and what they will say or why, these thoughts interfere with the original message. These preexisting ideas are impossible to eliminate, so communicators should be aware of their existence and consider these distractions and how they affect communication when they speak with others (Velentzas & Broni, 2014).

If, for example, an occupational therapist meets a colleague who has many tattoos and pink hair, he may ignore the conversation and conclude that she is unreliable because he does not like people who have tattoos and flashy hair. He decoded none of her messages. On the other hand, she may think he understood her message because she perceived from his body language that he was paying attention. In this real-life example, the content of the message was a significant change in the condition of a patient they were treating as a team, so the message given during the conversation was lost because of the OT's preconceptions about his colleague. This noise interfered with optimal services and outcomes for the patient.

Physical and Environmental Noise

The sounds of recreational and industrial work, roads, railroads, airports, and clusters of people produce physical and environmental noise that interferes with communication. External or environmental stimuli distract the person receiving the message (Velentzas & Broni, 2014). Examples of physical and environmental noise are background noises from a train or highway, music, or nearby conversations that make hearing challenging. This type of noise is relatively easy to identify and efforts to control it should be executed to promote good communication among the healthcare team.

Semantic Noise

Semantic noise happens when the language used by the sender/encoder of the message is unclear, has grammar mistakes, or is too technical (Velentzas & Broni, 2014). The receiver may not understand the message. The noise is caused by the sender when their word choice does not effectively convey the message (Velentzas & Broni, 2014). This is a common mistake made by health professionals who choose to use expertise-specific language with the people around them. Health professionals should take special care to be aware of semantic noise and avoid using medical jargon that is difficult for a layperson to understand.

Physiological Impairment Noise

Physiological impairment noise happens when physical disabilities such as blindness, deafness, or other medical conditions interfere with message content and interpretation (Velentzas & Broni, 2014). It can be caused by anyone involved in the communication process. For example, people with short-term memory loss or attention deficits may lose parts of the message or forget it during a conversation. In these cases, asking for the receiver's feedback to confirm their understanding or having them repeat the message in their own words can be good alternatives to solve the issue.

Syntactical Noise

Syntax and grammar mistakes in the message can break up communication; incorrect word order and language mistakes in verb tense cause syntactical noise (Velentzas & Broni, 2014). Incorrect use of language interrupts communication and distracts the receiver of the message, who will try to correct the message internally or feel that the incorrect language use is annoying. The message's sender may prevent syntactical noise by planning their communication before speaking up. A way to address syntactical noise is when the receiver speaks up and asks the sender to repeat the message using other words.

Organizational Noise

The life and success of an organization depend on effective communication (Velentzas & Broni, 2014). Organizational noise happens when the organization's policies, hierarchies, mission, vision, objectives, specific roles, and responsibilities of the employees are not clear, which results in poorly structured communication (Velentzas & Broni, 2014). Examples of these situations are unclear directions about operational changes or updates, lack of communication when new policies are established, and closed-doors management. When employees don't know what is expected from them or with whom to communicate, this can result in confusion during communication elements such as encoding, decoding, and feedback.

Cultural Noise

Cultural noise happens when people of different cultures, languages, and values communicate (Velentzas & Broni, 2014). It is expected that people who come from different cultures will interpret body language and words differently. Being aware of cultural differences and the communication issues that they may cause is the key to managing cultural noise. Senders should ensure the receiver understands their message by asking for feedback to prevent incorrect interpretations. The receiver can ask for clarification if they do not understand the sender's message.

Communication Barriers Within a Team

To optimize communication within a team, communication noises and barriers that happen should be identified (Velentzas & Broni, 2014). When noise and barriers are present, the communication cycle may be interrupted, the message may not be interpreted correctly by the receiver, or the words chosen by the sender may not be the best ones (Velentzas & Broni, 2014). Attention and understanding of the communication processes are key to preventing communication failures and mistakes. Frequent meetings to discuss, review, and analyze clinical cases emphasizing the communication purpose, elements, and cycle will optimize communication and promote team success.

System Design Barriers

Different systems are used in organizations to communicate. The hierarchical characteristics of the organization and its policies should facilitate communication. If the organizational structure is not clear, its employees will be confused as to whom to communicate regarding the different situations that happen daily (Velentzas & Broni, 2014). Inappropriate information, lack of training or supervision, and unclear responsibilities and roles can result in communication failures since the employees do not know enough about their jobs.

Attitudinal Barriers

Negative attitudes can happen as a result of staff problems in the organization. Situations such as poor management, lack of communication with employees, personality conflicts, lack of motivation, insufficient training, job dissatisfaction, payment delays, and resistance to change may result in people delays and refusals to communicate (Velentzas & Broni, 2014). Staffing problems, chronic lack of human resources, overwork, the absence of raises in salaries, shortage of health professionals, burnout, and excess of patients can increase stress for healthcare workers and cause chronic negativity and discomfort. These factors need to be addressed by administration and human resources to alleviate the stressors of the team, facilitate communication, and promote optimal outcomes.

Physical Barriers

Environmental obstacles, such as staff in different buildings, poor or obsolete equipment, and lack of new technological systems to facilitate the work, can cause physical barriers to communication. Poor lighting, background noise, and too cold or too hot environments can affect people's morale and ability to concentrate (Velentzas & Broni, 2014). Organizations should consider all these environmental factors to optimize communication processes among their staff.

Reflective Analysis: Communication Error Scenario

If there was a problem with one of the elements of communication and patient outcomes were not accomplished, analyzing, and reflecting using Kolb's Experiential Learning Perspective (Kolb, 1984; McLeod, 2024a) on the communication cycle can help you identify the mistakes and prevent communication errors in the future. The cycle, combined with the learning perspective, can be applied to analyze the communication experience and make it tangible and practical. In addition, Maslow's Hierarchy of Needs may be integrated into the analysis to continue the learning quest.

Mario's Case

A physical therapist (PT), Mario, needs to talk to the auditor, a nurse named Cristina, RN, but is in a hurry to visit a patient to get to lunch on time (he is diabetic and needs to eat food at certain times to prevent low glucose and a dizzy spell). The PT, in a hurry, does not plan his words; the nurse interprets his message as rude. The scenario is the following:

❧ KOLB'S LEARNING PERSPECTIVE STAGES ❧

1) **Concrete Experience**
   Mario, the PT, needs to talk to the auditor, Cristina, RN, to clarify a documentation incongruence she discovered in his clinical note. Cristina called him the day before because he wrote that the patient was chairfast, but in the evaluation tool, he wrote that he could walk. The incongruence must be fixed before sending the record to the Centers for Medicare & Medicaid Services (CMS); if the record submission is noncompliant, it cannot be uploaded to CMS. Cristina's purpose

is to fix the incongruence. Mario goes to her office to discuss the case. He looks worried and is fidgeting. Mario says, "What do you need from me?" Cristina repeats what she said on the phone the day before: "I found an incongruence in your documentation about the patient. Is the patient walking or chairfast?" He responds, "Can you please not call me while I am working in the field? You interrupted my work. The patient can walk only very short distances. What is the problem with that?" Cristina says, "I cannot have a chairfast patient who ambulates. Can you decide and change the record accordingly? What does the patient do most of his time?" Mario answers, "Mostly chairfast," and leaves. Cristina feels upset.

2) **Reflective Observation**
   The PT gave the RN the needed information for the record, but the communication was not smooth. Cristina felt upset after the meeting. This is an example of how tone and nonverbal communication can make the message uncomfortable for both clinicians. His nonverbal communication rushed the message, making the nurse feel unimportant, and his harsh attitude and wording did not help.

3) **Abstract Conceptualization**
   a. What happened? The communication transferred the needed information, but the process was unpleasant.
   b. What went wrong? Mario, the PT, was in a hurry, had low sugar levels, and used a harsh tone and words when speaking with the auditor, Cristina.
   c. What should they do next time to prevent miscommunication? Mario was in a hurry and should have taken his lunch before or clarified to Cristina why he was rushing. He could have spoken nicely or called back to apologize after his lunch.
   d. How can they improve communication within the team? Invite the clinicians to a communication workshop to improve communication skills and attitudes.

4) **Active Experimentation**
   Next time, try to communicate with a positive attitude and be polite. It was nobody's fault that the PT was in a hurry and had low glucose levels.

Communication Styles: The Personal Experience

Learning about communication styles will help you identify the type you prefer, understand how you communicate, and perceive how you may come across to others. Self-awareness of your flaws and strengths is essential in optimizing your communication with the people around you. Identifying and comprehending how your colleagues communicate can enhance your communication processes to reach the goals of your team. You can use different styles or a combination of them depending on the situation, but usually, people have a dominant communication style. On the internet, you can find many questionnaires and theories about communication styles. You will find different communication style articles in the Further Reading section at the end of this chapter.

Being a part of so many different healthcare professional teams for more than thirty-five years, I decided to create my own list of communication styles within healthcare teams. The key to this learning experience about communication is identifying, reflecting on, and analyzing diverse communication styles and experiences to assess and plan for future situations using Kolb's Experiential Learning Perspective (Kolb, 1984; McLeod, 2024a). In addition, Maslow's Hierarchy of Needs (Maslow, 1943; Maslow, 1954; McLeod, 2024b) will be integrated into the analysis. Each communication style will have its primary need—the person's main communication goal—identified. By identifying the primary needs of the members of your team at work, you may start opening their receptivity to communication by satisfying their needs first. This action can increase their communication motivation. It is by giving them positive reinforcement at the beginning of the communication process that you may open their minds to your message.

Through careful observation of and participation in different health professional teams, I have identified the following communication styles:

> ⌇ **Always in a Hurry**
> The main goal of this clinician is to get through their work as soon as possible. They want to get out of the office or situation fast. They communicate with half sentences using body language that expresses their rush. They pace, fidget, and even talk in a fast manner. They want to get over with every process quickly. PRIMARY NEED: To finish their tasks quickly.
> MASLOW'S HIERARCHY OF NEEDS: Safety and security.
> FACILITATE COMMUNICATION: Start by offering help with a task they need to do to open their communication "door." For example, helping them find documentation papers, pens, or pencils.

➤ **Bossy/Always Right**

Feel they know the truth and have 100 percent of the knowledge about every topic. They are not interested in hearing other members of the team's perspectives. Mostly closed to other team members' ideas and usually interpret messages from a biased perspective. Disagreement with them makes other team members their target for "revenge." Often feel insecure, so they must overcompensate.

PRIMARY NEED: To demonstrate that they are correct and that other team members do not understand the issue discussed. Feel insecure.

MASLOW'S HIERARCHY OF NEEDS: Safety and security.

FACILITATE COMMUNICATION: Show positive nonverbal cues such as assenting with your head and eye contact, then introduce your message.

➤ **Helper/Pleaser/Server**

They mostly agree with the group's efforts and work. They participate little during team meetings; they enjoy agreeing and collaborating with the group.

PRIMARY NEED: To please others and make friends.

MASLOW'S HIERARCHY OF NEEDS: Love and Belonging.

FACILITATE COMMUNICATION: Accept their help and show gratitude.

➤ **Silent/Dissident/Protester**

They find faults in teamwork goals and efforts but do not speak up. Complain about processes but provide no contributions. Engage in passive-aggressive behavior that is nonproductive and sometimes originates communication problems due to their biased interpretations.

PRIMARY NEED: To find faults and errors in team members' ideas. Worry about their own work's effectiveness. Feel insecure.

MASLOW'S HIERARCHY OF NEEDS: Safety and security.

FACILITATE COMMUNICATION: Ask them to speak up openly and find an opportunity to allow them to speak. For example, you can say their name and ask for their perspective during a meeting. Use reassuring language such as, "I would like to hear your perspective about this topic. We value your opinion."

➤ **Urchin Communicator**

Task-oriented. Communicate strictly to get what they need. Do not feel like part of the team. Think the team should work for them and provide fast solutions so they can achieve their tasks quickly. They do not hesitate to complain publicly about mistakes made by other team members if they interfere with or cause a delay in their work.

PRIMARY NEED: To complete their daily tasks and eliminate every distraction or delay.

MASLOW'S HIERARCHY OF NEEDS: Safety and security.

FACILITATE COMMUNICATION: Offer help with some of their tasks first and be kind (i.e., "Kill them with kindness").

➤ **Assertive Communicator**

Their purpose is to seek the truth and find solutions to the daily challenges of the team. They wait for their turn to speak up and use their voice in a positive and productive way. True collaborators!

PRIMARY NEED: Collaboration and successful teamwork.

MASLOW'S HIERARCHY OF NEEDS: Self-esteem and self-actualization.

FACILITATE COMMUNICATION: No facilitation is needed; they are natural and effective communicators. They get motivation from their self-awareness and strive to do their best.

Kolb's Learning Styles

Kolb's Theory of Learning identifies four learning styles (Kolb, 1984; McLeod, 2024a). Understanding learning styles can help with optimizing communication skills. The styles are diverging, assimilating, converging, and accommodating (Kolb, 1984; McLeod, 2024a). Kolb understood that every person has their favorite learning style and that understanding it will facilitate the learning process. Learning happens by feeling, watching, thinking, and doing, which are the basic actions described by Kolb's Learning Cycle. The cycle has four continuum stages where the learners prefer using a combination that can change depending on the situation (Kolb, 1984; McLeod, 2024a). Learners who prefer to feel and watch use the diverging style. With the assimilating style, learners think and watch. Learners use the converging style to think and do and the accommodating style to feel and do.

Review Figure 1 (pg. 13) for a visual depiction of Kolb's Learning Styles.

Diverging *(Feeling and Watching – Concrete Experience/Reflective Observation)*

Diverging learners are sensitive and can view situations from different perspectives (Kolb, 1984; McLeod, 2024a). They are interested in people and enjoy gathering information by observing and using their imagination to solve issues. They observe concrete situations and can consider different viewpoints. They like brainstorming, have different cultural interests, and enjoy gathering information.

Assimilating *(Watching and Thinking – Abstract Conceptualization/Reflective Observation)*

Assimilating learners use logic; ideas and theories are more important than people to them. They prefer learning through detailed explanations, which they organize logically (Kolb, 1984; McLeod, 2024a). They enjoy conferences, readings, exploring, and thinking about what they learn. People with this learning style are successful in science and information careers (Kolb, 1984; McLeod, 2024a).

Converging *(Doing and Thinking – Abstract Conceptualization/Active Experimentation)*

Converging learners like to find practical solutions to solve problems and answer questions (Kolb, 1984; McLeod, 2024a). They are more concerned with completing assignments and tasks than worrying about people and relationships. They enjoy experimentation with new concepts, simulation, and working with pragmatic applications. People with this learning style are successful in using their technological abilities.

Accommodating *(Doing and Feeling – Concrete Experience/Active Experimentation)*

Accommodating learners like having a hands-on experience that relies on intuition (Kolb, 1984; McLeod, 2024a). They go through the learning experience by doing an activity and putting plans into concrete practice. They get information from others instead of doing their own analysis process. This is the most common learning style in the population.

Optimizing Communication and Preventing Communication Errors

In summary, understanding the specifics of communication is key to optimizing the communication process. These include the communication cycle and its components, the message, the purpose of the communicator, what makes communication effective, communication styles and noise, and the skills needed to communicate effectively. Frequent team meetings to reflect on and analyze communication failures can help improve the communication processes and the team's daily rapport and well-being. When people can identify a safe space to share their working goals and ideas about improving teamwork, it can result in better communication, thus optimizing patient outcomes and facilitating the organization's success. It's important to discuss different cases that involved failed communication so you can understand how it affected patients' outcomes and how to improve for the future. Kolb's Experiential Learning Perspective (Kolb, 1984; McLeod, 2024a) and the template in Appendix A can be used as a meeting guide. In addition, written records should be kept as evidence and compared with future cases to display the team's effort and improvement.

Educational Activities

This section is an integral part of the learning journey throughout the book. These activities and hands-on exercises will encourage you to reflect and consider more profound personal experiences. Perform each activity carefully to optimize the results of your communication skills. You can execute the learning activities individually, in pairs, or with your professional team. To facilitate the activities, a template was designed to be printed by the readers. It can be used as a visual-motor aid when working on communication examples. The template is included in Appendix A.

Group Discussion: How Communication Mistakes Can Affect Patient Outcomes

a. Think about real-life communication mistakes that affected patient outcomes. Remember the event and discuss what happened. Create two examples, reflect, and discuss with the group what could have been done differently to improve communication and patient outcomes in similar situations. Go back to Kolb's Experiential Learning Theory to identify the process. Remember the experience, reflect, analyze, and practice.

b. Recall past experiences of ineffective communication, thinking about the communication cycle and the components of communication. Remember what happened and take notes. Create two examples, reflect, and discuss with the group what components made the communication ineffective. Go back to Kolb's Experiential Learning Theory. Remember the experience, reflect, analyze, and plan for future conditions.

c. Remember, reflect, explain, analyze, and create examples to understand how communication mistakes affect patient outcomes. What are the results of communication errors?

Reflection Points

➤ Give examples of typical communication errors that take place among your team.

➤ Describe complex patient cases in which clinical judgment errors happened because of communication mistakes. Analyze communication elements. Then, think about how to prevent judgment errors in the future.

➤ Identify and reflect on the most common communication noises you experience daily. Are they psychological, physical, semantic, environmental, physiological impairment, syntactical, organizational, or cultural? You can categorize them from the ones that affect you the most to those that affect you the least.

➤ Consider how you can remove different communication noises.

➤ Do you feel you pay enough attention to your colleagues when they speak to you at work? If not, can you think of strategies to pay more attention to them?

➤ Describe ways in which you can improve your communication skills.

➤ Can you identify your main communication style? Remember, you can use different styles or a combination of them depending on the situation. The styles are: Always in a Hurry, Urchin Communicator, Assertive Communicator, Bossy/Always Right, Helper/Pleaser/Server, Silent/Dissident/Protester.

➤ Identify and think about your team members who use different communication styles. Think about your experiences with them. How can you improve your communication with them?

➤ Identify your learning style. Is it diverging, assimilating, converging, or accommodating? Which is your weakest style? Identifying your less-preferred styles can help you design practice experiences by applying Experiential Learning, as explained by Kolb.

As you read other chapters, you can return to these examples and situations to assess your learning process and see if you can solve the situations differently. In addition, you can remember other experiences from your past using the template in Appendix A. Practice will promote deeper understanding and improve your communication skills. Perform the method for different cases.

Further Reading

1) *Different styles of communication.* (2015, February 8). Daily Herald [Arlington Heights, IL], 13. https://0b30ikngx-mp02-y-https-link-gale-com.prxusa. lirn.net/apps/doc/A400850505/STND?u=lirn55718&sid=bookmark-ST-ND&xid=af1658b3.

2) Dhillon, N., & Kaur, G. (2023). *Impact of Personality Traits on Communication Effectiveness of Teachers: Exploring the Mediating Role of Their Communication Style.* SAGE Open, 13(2). https://doi.org/10.1177/21582440231168049.

3) García-Ramírez., J.M. (2012). *Communication, key to visible excellence in Higher Education.* Journal for Educators, Teachers and Trainers, 3, 25–36. http://www.ugr.es/~jett/pdf/vol03_02_jett_garcia-ramirez.pdf.

4) Mohamed, M., & Zainal Abidin, K. (2021). *Principals' Communication Styles and School Culture in Vocational Colleges in Selangor.* Asian Journal of University Education, 17(4), 24–34.

5) McLeod, S. (2024a, February 2). *Kolb's learning styles and experiential learning cycle.* Simply Psychology. https://www.simplypsychology.org/learning-kolb.html.

6) Sergy, L. (2017). *What is communication?* In Handy Answer: The Handy Communication Answer Book. Visible Ink Press. Retrieved September 18, 2023, from https://search.credoreference.com/es/articles/Qm9va0Fy-dGljbGU6NDMyMzQyMg==

CHAPTER THREE

---◦---

Communication Barriers:
Causes and Solutions

Communication Barriers: Causes and Solutions

To understand ineffective communication, the etiology of communication barriers needs to be studied and analyzed. Exploring the background and impact of communication blocks in the healthcare team on real cases will bring relevance to this learning experience. Enhancing communication improves clinical documentation, reduces problematic accreditation findings, avoids cost increases, prevents costly remedial actions, and ensures patient beneficence.

Therefore, the ethical aspect of optimizing teamwork to improve patients' health should motivate every healthcare professor, clinician, and student to strive for successful communication. The causes of communication barriers are 1) Behavioral, 2) Cognitive, 3) Linguistic, 4) Environmental, and 5) Technological (Guttman et al., 2021). Chapter three will identify the different causal barriers to communication and introduce specific recommendations to improve related communication patterns in the future. It is important to note that in real situations, barriers to communication can be mixed.

In chapter two, communication was defined as a reciprocal process between the people who send and receive information. Internal and external factors influence communication processes (Salas et al., 2014). Communication affects the behaviors, thoughts, and attitudes of those communicating (Gephart & Cholette, 2012; Guttman et al., 2021; Salas et al., 2014). The quest to discover communication barriers and their solutions through reading and deep analysis of past communication experiences will facilitate communication optimization. Learning from previous experiences is essential to implementing focused efforts to improve communication among a healthcare team.

Behavioral Barriers

A **behavioral barrier** is a lack of communication when someone does not speak up (Guttman et al., 2021). Speaking up is when you voice thoughts out loud using verbal communication that is heard by others. Speaking up is the opposite of remaining silent. Sometimes, clinicians do not speak up for fear of being incorrect or perceived as incapable or incompetent (Guttman et al., 2021). Another behavioral issue is the desire to avoid past negative experiences (Milliken & Morrison, 2003).

Solutions

To promote speak up behavior among an interprofessional team, you need to build members' trust. People speak up when they perceive an atmosphere of psychological safety (Edmondson, 1999). Evidence has demonstrated that power balance among the members of an interprofessional team ensures good communication, collaboration, coordination, and mutual responsibility (Engum & Jeffries, 2012; Hazarika, 2019; McDonald et al., 2012; Okpala, 2021). Managers can promote power balance through collaboration, education, mentoring and direct communication, education, and open-door policies (Okpala, 2021). Workshops and activities can be used to build the team's trust; examples include relational coordination, events to fraternize (Guttman et al., 2021) and teaching Medical Improv, during which the participants practice theater techniques to improve teamwork and communication (Boynton, 2022; Guttman et al., 2021; Kukora et al., 2020; Mehta et al., 2020; Watson & Fu, 2016). Another approach to improve communication is to schedule short, daily, goal-oriented, structured communication meetings known as huddles or briefs with the team (Royse et al., 2020). These routine communications give team members the opportunity to update their mental models while facilitating daily interaction (Royse et al., 2020). Effective communication takes practice. Getting into the habit of short daily team meetings can eventually build team members' trust and encourage them to speak up.

Reflective Analysis: Behavioral Barrier Scenario

To analyze a behavioral communication barrier, an actual situation within an interprofessional team will be used. The team members were two auditors who were also nurses and a physical therapist. Kolb's Experiential Learning Perspective (Kolb, 1984; McLeod, 2024a) will be used to analyze the case, and then Maslow's Hierarchy of Needs (McLeod, 2024b) will be applied to support optimized communication.

Interprofessional Team Meeting Case

☙ KOLB'S LEARNING PERSPECTIVE STAGES ❧

1) **Concrete Experience**
   Jane, the clinical manager, scheduled a meeting at a round table in her office to discuss her findings regarding the accuracy

of the auditor's work for the last month. Both auditors, Carla and Denise, attended. During the meeting, Jane congratulated the team because the results revealed 96 percent accuracy by both auditors, which was a significant success. In addition, Jane revealed that some errors were discovered and discussed them in detail. The mistakes had been made by Carla, who remained silent and was visibly sweating during the meeting. Denise spoke about her own performance and made some suggestions regarding the errors found. Jane, the manager, congratulated both auditors and ended the meeting. During the afternoon, Carla requested a private meeting with Jane to explain that she had felt uncomfortable during the meeting because she was the one responsible for the mistakes. She expressed to Jane that she would try to improve her performance. Jane told Carla that her performance was 96 percent accurate, that she should feel free to speak up during the meetings, and that a mistake can happen to anyone. She expressed that her office is and will always be open to Carla to voice her concerns and perspectives and invited her to come back to her office whenever she feels the need.

2) **Reflective Observation**

The meeting accomplished its goal of analyzing the audit team's performance, but Carla felt uncomfortable after realizing that the only mistakes discovered during the manager's audit were hers. She remained silent during the whole meeting, which was evidence that she did not feel psychologically safe to speak up.

3) **Abstract Conceptualization**

    a.   What happened? Jane, the manager, communicated the information she needed to the auditors, but the process was unpleasant for Carla, the auditor who committed the mistakes.

    b.   What went wrong? After hearing the results, the auditors could deduce who had committed the mistakes. Carla identified that she was responsible for the mistakes that were discussed. Carla felt uncomfortable and not psychologically safe to speak up during the meeting.

    c.   What should they do next time to prevent miscommunication? The manager should not mention the results specifically so the members of the team can feel psychologically safe to speak up, and those who made mistakes do not feel exposed to the rest of the team.

    d.   How can they improve communication within the team? In the future, discuss findings without being specific.

Invite the clinicians to a communication workshop to improve communication.

4) **Active Experimentation**

Next time, the manager should plan how she is going to discuss her findings. Discussing the results of audits in a way that those in the meeting cannot identify who committed the mistakes may make the team members feel more comfortable and psychologically safe to speak up during the meetings.

✺ Maslow's Hierarchy of Needs ✺

Carla felt uncomfortable during the meeting. Carla needed to feel psychologically safe to be able to speak up. In Maslow's Hierarchy of Needs, the second stage, safety needs, includes personal security, resources, health, property, and employment (McLeod, 2024b). The manager must facilitate those safety needs during team meetings and daily work by establishing that the meetings are safe spaces to communicate.

Cognitive Barriers

Cognitive barriers to communication happen when the message is interrupted, lacks information or context, or has unnecessary and distracting information (Guttman et al., 2021). The information is not carried from sender to receiver properly, interfering with understanding and attention levels. These barriers can include distractions and interruptions for both senders and receivers, making it difficult to perceive and process the message (Guttman et al., 2021). Environmental barriers which will be discussed later, are different from cognitive barriers in that they are physical noises that interrupt the message. Environmental barriers can cause cognitive barriers that affect message interpretation because they distract the people having a conversation. Cognitive and environmental barriers can be related and mixed in real-life situations.

Solutions

To avoid cognitive barriers and increase attention to communication, create a "sterile-cockpit" environment, avoiding unnecessary talk, human traffic, noises, and alarms in the workplace (Guttman et al., 2021) because they interfere with message interpretation. Understanding and sharing the responsibility of clear communication within the team is another way to decrease cognitive barriers. Empathy and humor can aid in communication between the team (Giroldi et al.,

2015). Another way to optimize information sharing is using a communication template such as Situation, Background, Assessment, and Recommendation known as SBAR, which the US Navy created (Narayan, 2013). Using the SBAR can increase communication effectiveness and the speed of information sharing during case discussions, emails, and internal memos to inform patient status (Guttman et al., 2021). It is essential to know that communication barriers can be mixed in different situations. For example, environmental barriers such as noises interfere with message understanding, causing a distraction or interruption, which are the cognitive barriers discussed in this section.

Reflective Analysis: Cognitive Barrier Scenario

An actual situation will be used to analyze a cognitive communication barrier. The team members are a physical therapist (PT) and three nurses. Kolb's Experiential Learning Perspective (Kolb, 1984; McLeod, 2024a) and Maslow's Hierarchy of Needs (McLeod, 2024b) will be applied to the process. Performing a deep analysis of this communication situation is an effective way to continue the learning process about communication barriers and how to overcome them.

The Audit That Needed to Be Submitted for Payment in Thirty Minutes

⪜ KOLB'S LEARNING PERSPECTIVE STAGES ⪛

1) **Concrete Experience**
   The team needed to discuss a case to help the clinical nurse, Adriana, and the auditor nurse, Ivelisse, complete an audit quickly to submit the case for payment. It was the last day to upload the case according to the payer's regulations before the agency started to lose a percentage of the payment for the services. The case needed to be solved in thirty minutes or less for upload. The PT, Mara, was called by Ivelisse as a mediator because the other nurse, the services coordinator, Neisa, was already upset by a communication failure with Adriana. The PT had to leave in ten minutes to visit a patient. Ivelisse explained that the medical orders of the case were not aligned with the case data and needed to be changed. Neisa explained that she had told Adriana to call the physician during the original case discussion thirty days ago, and Adriana had not made the call. Mara told Neisa to repeat herself because she could

not understand her. Neisa was using too many words and speaking very loudly in the heat of the moment. In addition, there was noise in the office nearby because some of the staff were talking loudly about some other work situation. Mara called Adriana by phone to discuss the case. Adriana commented that she was sick and tired of Neisa using texts to communicate. Adriana explained that she had discussed the case with the patient's physician earlier that day, and the physician had told her that she would sign the new orders so the services could be continued. Mara calmly explained what Adriana had said to Ivelisse and Neisa. Together, they prepared new physician's orders to be signed by the physician to complete the case audit. The case was solved and submitted in time for upload.

2) **Reflective Observation**

The meeting goal was accomplished, as the audit team submitted the case on time. However, all the team members were uncomfortable with the situation. The communication block could have been prevented with timely communication between the services coordinator and the clinical nurse.

3) **Abstract Conceptualization**

    a.   What happened? The case discussion and mediation by the physical therapist provided the needed audit information, but the process was unpleasant for the team. They were working against the clock.

    b.   What went wrong? There was a communication failure between the services coordinator nurse and the clinical nurse thirty days before the audit.

    c.   What should they do next time to prevent miscommunication? The services coordinator should follow up in a timely fashion regarding the case pending new physician's orders. She should schedule a weekly meeting to solve incomplete cases before sending them for the audit process.

    d.   How can they improve communication among the team? Invite the clinicians to a communication workshop to improve communication. Create fraternization activities to increase bonds within the interprofessional team.

4) **Active Experimentation**

Next time, the services coordinator will follow up on all the incomplete cases before submitting them for the audit process. This action should prevent the lack of aligned medical orders in the future.

≈ Maslow's Hierarchy of Needs ≈

The team felt uncomfortable with the situation mainly because of the time constraint. The services coordinator and the clinical nurse were significantly affected by the communication failure. The case needed to be uploaded in thirty minutes to comply with regulations. This situation relates to the second level of Maslow's Hierarchy, safety needs for personal security, resources, health, property, and employment (McLeod, 2024b). In this case, the team needed to protect the payment to the agency that pays the team. Timely work and better scheduling to follow up on incomplete cases would satisfy their safety needs effectively.

Linguistic Barriers

Communication failure caused by problems with the components of speech and its structure are known as **linguistic barriers** (Guttman et al., 2021). Elements include speech style, tone, word order and choice, rhythm, speed, voice fluctuations, word meaning, metaphors, jargon, idioms, grammar, context, and similar-sounding words (Guttman et al., 2021). How people speak and deliver a message impacts the communication. Using technical terms or medical jargon that people without expertise cannot understand is a linguistic issue. Utilizing figures of speech about topics the message receivers cannot understand also causes linguistic barriers (Guttman et al., 2021).

Solutions

To prevent linguistic barriers to communication, speakers and listeners should confirm their message was understood by verifying with the receiver or asking for feedback after communication happens (Guttman et al., 2021). For example, after relaying the message, the speaker should ask the listener if they understood or need clarification. In addition, the speaker can repeat the message using different word choices. Some people do not speak up for fear of asking "stupid" questions. Therefore, the speaker should state that no question is stupid or unnecessary. It is essential to make the listener feel safe. The final message is the one that the listener fully understands.

Reflective Analysis: Linguistic Barrier Scenario

To analyze a linguistic communication barrier, one of the most common among health professionals will be used. It is the use of jargon when speaking up. The team members are a speech language pathologist (SLP), José, and a nurse auditor, Joyce, during a case discussion. Kolb's Experiential Learning Perspective (Kolb, 1984; McLeod, 2024a) and Maslow's Hierarchy of Needs (McLeod, 2024b) will be used to analyze and continue the active learning process about communication barriers and how to defeat them.

Technical Jargon During a Case Discussion

⁂ KOLB'S LEARNING PERSPECTIVE STAGES ⁂

1) **Concrete Experience**
   The auditor, Joyce, needed to discuss a case with the SLP, José, to clarify his perspective on the primary diagnosis of a patient who had a stroke. Other clinicians had documented their principal diagnosis, but the SLP had not. Joyce called to ask José about the diagnosis. He explained using anatomical and technical language that Joyce did not understand. Joyce stopped José, saying, "Can you use other words to describe the patient's speech dysfunction so I can understand you?" José apologized and explained the diagnoses using common words, saying that the patient was having difficulty swallowing due to oropharyngeal dysfunction and receptive aphasia. Joyce thanked José for the clarification.

2) **Reflective Observation**
   The auditor achieved her goal for the discussion, but the SLP needed to be aware of using a common language with the team so that everyone can understand each other. This could have been prevented by using clear and straightforward vocabulary.

3) **Abstract Conceptualization**
   a. What happened? José was using technical language that Joyce could not understand, which made the conversation difficult.
   b. What went wrong? There was a short communication failure between José and Joyce. She felt psychologically safe to give José her feedback about not understanding his jargon, which he immediately corrected using a common vocabulary from then on.
   c. What should they do next time to prevent miscommunication? José should be aware that some of his language is complex for other health professionals. He needs to find a common language for everyone in the team.

d. How can they improve communication within the team?
Invite the clinicians to a workshop about communication
barriers to improve communication. Create fraternized
activities to increase bonds among the interprofessional team.

4) **Active Experimentation**
Next time, José will be more aware of the language he's using.
He will find common words to use with the team. Joyce has
good speak up behavior; she quickly voiced her thoughts when
she could not understand José. She should continue speaking up
and encourage others to do the same.

⚞ Maslow's Hierarchy of Needs ⚟

The case felt uncomfortable for Joyce because she could not understand
José's technical language. She needed to understand him to be able to audit
the record and send it for payment, a process that has a time constraint.
This issue has to do with Maslow's second stage, safety needs, where a
person needs personal security, resources, health, property, and employment
(McLeod, 2024b). In this case, both members of the team needed to be able
to communicate effectively. Joyce asked for more familiar language. José
paraphrased his words to promote Joyce's understanding immediately. A
positive attitude and effective teamwork are practical and produce optimal
outcomes.

Environmental Barriers

The barriers caused by equipment, staff conversations, use of tools, machinery,
sounds, and alarms in the place where communication happens are called
environmental barriers (Hasfeldt et al., 2010). They are audible noises that
interfere with the transmission and or reception of the message. Environmental
barriers are connected to cognitive barriers because it is common for noise to
interfere with the interpretation and understanding of messages. When this
happens, an environmental barrier causes a cognitive barrier.

Solutions

To solve environmental barriers, attention should be given to the office
space. The division of space in an office environment should be designed
effectively to cut out as much noise as possible. In addition, masks and other
equipment should be purchased with communication in mind. For example,

buy masks with clear plastic windows so team members' faces and gestures will still be visible (Guttman et al., 2021).

Reflective Analysis: Environmental Barrier Scenario

An actual situation will be used to analyze an environmental communication barrier. The team members are two physical therapists (PTs), two nurses, and the billings director. To continue the quest for knowledge to defeat communication barriers, Kolb's Experiential Learning Perspective (Kolb, 1984; McLeod, 2024a) and Maslow's Hierarchy of Needs (McLeod, 2024b) will be applied to the analysis.

A Day of Street Construction and Repairs

⋙ Kolb's Learning Perspective Stages ⋘

1) **Concrete Experience**
   The team, composed of two nurses and two PTs, was called by Margaret, the director of the billing department, to discuss a case. She needed to finish a case to send it for payment for the services provided to the patient, but the clinicians had not completed the record documentation. The patient had received services from both the nursing and the PT departments. As soon as the discussion started, the street construction workers' machinery started to make a very high volume of constant noise, so the team could not hear each other. They decided to move the meeting to a closed room where they could hear each other. They were thankful that they had the opportunity to use a different meeting room and could discuss the case successfully.

2) **Reflective Observation**
   The meeting accomplished its goal of completing the billing process in time because team members handled the environmental barrier, changing the meeting to a room where the noises did not affect their communication process.

3) **Abstract Conceptualization**
   a. What happened? The team identified an environmental barrier; as soon as the noise started, they moved the meeting to the room where it could not be heard.
   b. What went wrong? There was a communication failure within the team because of environmental noise caused by the construction

work on the road nearby. The team identified the communication barrier and solved it by changing the meeting place.

  c. What should they do next time to prevent miscommunication? The team solved the communication barrier effectively and quickly. Healthcare teams are always working against the clock and must be creative and productive to solve any communication issue.

  d. How can they improve communication within the team? There is always room for improvement. The agency should invite the clinicians to a communication workshop to improve communication. Create fraternized activities to increase bonds among the interprofessional team.

4) **Active Experimentation**
  The team should be aware of communication barriers so they can solve them, which will increase productivity and effectiveness in the health professionals' team.

⚞ Maslow's Hierarchy of Needs ⚟

The team felt uncomfortable with the noise situation caused by the construction. They solved the issue by changing the meeting to a room that was insulated against noise. All working activities should be productive to keep the agency economically healthy. Health services provided by different insurance companies have their own policies and time constraints. This concerns Maslow's second stage, safety needs, where the team needs personal security, resources, health, property, and employment (McLeod, 2024b). Every communication barrier affects productivity. They should be handled as priorities to promote optimal outcomes.

Technological Barriers

Technological barriers originate from electronic medical records (EMR), which can distract healthcare professionals from the patients or affect team communication negatively, slowing patient care and promoting illness (Guttman et al., 2021). When clinicians, faculty, and students have trouble looking for information in and uploading or downloading data to the EMR, it interferes with communication processes among staff and patients, even delaying clinical interventions (Guttman et al., 2021). Furthermore, the format of the EMR separates provider notes, which has a negative impact on the detection of critical illness and can potentially affect patients' health (Hoonakker et al., 2013).

Another technological issue is brought about by texting in group chats, which is a common way for health professional teams to communicate throughout the day. These group chats involve documentation findings, new policies, coordinating patient visits, professional appointments, education, or other valid professional purposes that are part of work. Even so, they often interrupt face-to-face interactions with patients, their caregivers, and the clinical team. These interruptions may cause other communication barriers, such as behavioral, cognitive, and environmental, because they disrupt the clinician's mindset during their interventions.

Solutions

To avoid technological barriers to communication, clinicians must be aware of how technology interrupts communication. They should fully understand the EMR system before treating patients and maximize their interaction with them by making eye contact and letting the patient look at their chart (Guttman et al., 2021). Additionally, clinicians should explain to patients what they do with the EMR and discontinue interruptions by logging off when they're done charting (Guttman et al., 2021). In the case of group chats, they should not be used while providing clinical interventions.

Reflective Analysis: Technological Barrier Scenario

An actual situation will be used to analyze a technological communication barrier. The team members are a physical therapist (PT) and the clinical coordinator, a nurse who assigns the patients to the clinicians daily. Kolb's Experiential Learning Perspective (Kolb, 1984; McLeod, 2024a) and Maslow's Hierarchy of Needs (McLeod, 2024b) will be used for analysis to continue the learning process about communication barriers and how to overcome them.

Visiting a Patient While Getting Priority Messages from the Clinical Coordinator

⇜ KOLB'S LEARNING PERSPECTIVE STAGES ⇝

1) **Concrete Experience**
   The PT, María, arrived at the patient's home. As soon as she arrived, messages from the clinical coordinator, Carmen, started

arriving on her cell phone and making very loud notification sounds. Before starting the intervention, María explained to the patient that she would not start the evaluation process until she answered the messages from work that were important. The messages were about the PT forgetting to visit another patient assigned three weeks before. She answered the initial message, but the nurse kept sending more messages, and the notification sounds interrupted the admission process. The patient said, "You need to tell the nurse that she is interrupting your work with me." María apologized and silenced the cell phone to continue working without interruptions. No other interruptions happened.

2) **Reflective Observation**

Repeated text messages with very loud sound notifications were interrupting the admission process for the patient and could have potentially interfered with the PT's thoughts and analysis if they'd continued. This could have caused not only a technological barrier but a cognitive one for the PT, who could have become confused or overwhelmed by the interruptions during the visit. In the future, the PT should mute notifications while visiting patients to prevent technological and cognitive barriers during interventions.

3) **Abstract Conceptualization**

a. What happened? Frequent text message notifications interfered with communication between the patient and María, the PT.

b. What went wrong? Too many priority messages were received by the PT during an admission visit.

c. What should they do next time to prevent miscommunication? The PT should mute text notifications and calls during patient visits to prevent communication interruptions with the patient.

d. How should they improve communication within the team? Explain how continuous text messaging interrupts clinicians' work and can cause technological and cognitive communication barriers. These can cause a suboptimal focus of the PT during the evaluation process and clinical judgment mistakes. Invite the clinicians to a communication workshop to improve communication. Create fraternization activities to increase bonds among the interprofessional team.

4) **Active Experimentation**

Next time, the PT will mute her cell phone notifications during patient's visits. The clinical coordinator should understand that the PT will answer her messages when they do not interfere with the patient's interventions.

⚞ MASLOW'S HIERARCHY OF NEEDS ⚟

The PT, Maria, felt uncomfortable because of the frequent interruptions of the text messages from the clinical coordinator as well as the argument about her supposed forgetfulness regarding a patient three weeks before. This situation concerns Maslow's second stage, safety needs, where the person needs personal security, resources, health, property, and employment (McLeod, 2024b). In this case, the PT needed to protect her integrity and truthfulness toward the clinical coordinator. Timely work and better communication between the PT and the clinical coordinator about scheduling patients' appointments for visits will prevent future situations. Similarly, the clinical coordinator should follow up on incomplete cases weekly to satisfy the team's safety needs and avoid interrupting future patient care.

Educational Activities

This section is an integral part of the learning journey throughout the book. These activities and hands-on exercises will encourage you to reflect and consider more profound personal experiences. Perform each activity carefully to optimize the results for your communication skills. You can execute the learning activities individually, in pairs, or with your professional team. To facilitate the activities, a template was designed to be printed by the readers. It can be used as a visual-motor aid when working on communication examples. The template is included in Appendix A.

Role-Playing: Design Scenarios

a. Think about real-life communication problems that you have had. Remember the experiences and note what happened. Think of an example of each communication barrier (behavioral, cognitive, linguistic, environmental, technological). Try to identify if more than one barrier was present in each situation. Reflect and discuss with a colleague what could have been done differently to improve communication. Go back to Kolb's Experiential Learning Perspective to identify each element of the process. Remember the experience, reflect, analyze, and practice.

b. Recall past experiences of ineffective communication within your team. Remember each one of the team member's contributions or communication blocks. Remember what happened and make notes. Which members of the team speak up? Who remains silent during meetings? Who speaks too fast, too slow, or uses jargon and difficult metaphors? Think of two examples, then reflect and discuss with a colleague which elements made the communication ineffective. Think about ways to improve communication among team members. Go back to Kolb's Experiential Learning Perspective. Remember the experience, reflect on it, analyze it, and plan for future situations.

c. Recall, reflect on, explain, and analyze examples about the benefits of effective communication. Go to the administrative sector of your job and explain how Medical Improv workshops, fraternization activities, and daily briefs would improve communication and trust within the team. Explain to them the results of good communication practices.

Reflection Points

➤ What communication barrier affects you the most?

➤ Identify the most common communication barriers that affect your team.

➤ Analyze the best way to improve communication within your team.

➤ Ask yourself if you understand everyone on your team when they speak. If there are people whom you usually do not understand, think about the following:

- Why can't you understand them?
- Do they speak too fast, speak too slow, slur their words, or use metaphors?
- Do they use difficult jargon?
- Is the environment full of noises that interfere with the messages?
- Consider ways to improve understanding within your team.

As you read other chapters, you can return to these examples to assess your learning process and see if you can solve the situations differently. In addition, you can analyze other experiences from your past using the template in Appendix A. Practice will promote deeper understanding and improve your communication skills.

Further Reading

1) Guttman, O. T., Lazzara, E. H., Keebler, J. R., Webster, K. L., Gisick, L. M., & Baker, A. L. (2021). *Dissecting communication barriers in healthcare: A path to enhancing communication resiliency, reliability, and patient safety.* Journal of Patient Safety, 17(8), e1465-e1471. https://doi.org/10.1097/pts.0000000000000541.

2) Boynton, B. [Beth Boynton]. (2022, February 16). *Introduction to Medical Improv for Leaders – Reinventing Communication & Culture in Healthcare.* [Video] YouTube. https://www.youtube.com/watch?v=u25fw_h4Zvg.

3) Edmondson, A. (1999). *Psychological safety and learning behavior in work teams.* Administrative Science Quarterly, 44(2), 350-383. https://doi.org/10.2307/2666999.

4) Hazarika, I. (2019). *Health workforce governance: Key to the delivery of people-centred care.* International Journal of Healthcare Management, 14(2), 358-362.https://doi.org/10.1080/20479700.2019.1647380.

5) Engum, S. A., & Jeffries, P. R. (2012). *Interdisciplinary collisions: Bringing healthcare professionals together.* Collegian, 19(3), 145-151. https://doi.org/10.1016/j.colegn.2012.05.00.

CHAPTER FOUR

Speak Up, Silence, and Voice Behaviors

Speak Up, Silence, and Voice Behaviors

Communication is when messages are sent by one party and received by another in the same physical or virtual environment, such as in the household, at school, online, in the community, and at work. Those who choose to communicate feel driven to share messages to accomplish a goal individually or with others while working together as a team. People must be motivated to communicate and strive to communicate effectively, especially at work, because their communication behaviors will have consequences. Communication can lead to progress, stagnation, or success.

In this chapter, the discussion will revolve around analyzing three communication actions: speak up, silence, and voice behaviors. Learning about these behaviors is essential to understanding and optimizing communication. As I went through the literature about these topics, I found that silence and voice behaviors have essential effects on individuals and the organizations they work for. These actions can direct how teams work and interact. In addition, these behaviors move the organization forward or even interfere with progress.

Health professionals must work as a cohesive team to provide optimal patient care (Carney et al., 2019; de Assis Brito et al., 2022; Nester, 2016; Pack et al., 2022; Ross et al., 2015; Royse et al., 2020). Careful and accurate communication among team members is vital for successful outcomes (de Assis Brito et al., 2022; Gutmann et al., 2021). Everyone who works values job security as a safety need; the second stage of Maslow's Hierarchy involves personal security, resources, employment, property, and money (Maslow, 1943; Maslow, 1954; McLeod, 2024b). A job is needed for an employee to ensure an income to support their lifestyle.

Moreover, individuals want to excel at their jobs, realize their professional aspirations, and move their organizations forward. These desires are related to Maslow's (Maslow, 1943; Maslow, 1954; McLeod, 2024b) fourth and fifth (final) stages. The fourth stage, esteem, represents respect, self-esteem, prestige, recognition, power, and independence. The fifth stage, self-actualization, reflects the desire to become the best person one can be (Maslow, 1943; Maslow, 1954; McLeod, 2024b).

Speak Up Behavior

Speak up behavior happens when someone talks or expresses messages to others in a face-to-face or virtual meeting. Health professionals should share questions and concerns about patients to other team members using their speak up behavior (Guttman et al., 2021; Lyndon et al., 2011). When people do not speak up, communication does not occur (Guttman et al., 2021).

The Effects of Speak Up Behavior

Speak up behavior results in communication and the sharing of ideas between health professionals in the team. Lack of speak up behavior results in absent or ineffective communication among the healthcare team. This lack of communication produces suboptimal patient care, including errors and adverse events (Lingard, 2004; Rabøl et al., 2011), and decreases patient safety (Guttman et al., 2021; Kohn et al., 2001; O'Donovan & McAuliffe, 2020a), thus interfering with patient outcomes. When people speak up, the constructive ideas they share can generate good individual outcomes and improvements in the workplace (Duan et al., 2019). Moreover, speaking up about mistakes improves learning, creativity, performance, and overall service (O'Donovan & McAuliffe, 2020a).

Silence Behavior

When a team member intentionally reserves information, thoughts, perspectives, or queries about an organization's issues and developments, it is called **silence behavior** (Dyne et al., 2003; Milliken et al., 2003b; Prouska & Psychogios, 2018). Silence behavior is inhibition-oriented to avoid social rejection or discomfort (Brinsfield, 2013; Kish-Gephart et al., 2009). People engage in this behavior to evade new negative situations (Elliot, 2006) and unwanted consequences (Carver, 2006; Morrison, See, & Pan, 2015).

Some people remain silent because they think their ideas are not valued or wanted by their superiors or top management (Morrison & Milliken, 2000). This silence results in a lack of interest and motivation. In these environments, conformism is promoted, and dissent is suppressed (Knoll & van Dick, 2013). It is essential to understand that silence behavior is a mindful decision the worker makes to suppress communication (Dyne et al., 2003; Milliken et al., 2003; Prouska & Psychogios, 2018).

Types of Silence Behavior

Silence behavior has four different forms: acquiescent, defensive, opportunistic, and prosocial, which differ depending upon the purpose or motive of the action (Knoll & van Dick, 2013). All types of silence behavior result in deliberately withholding information from the organization (Wu et al., 2023).

Acquiescent silence is the passive suppression of significant ideas that comes from feelings of resignation and submission (Knoll & van Dick, 2013; Pinder & Harlos, 2001). It is a disconnected behavior (Farrell, 1983; Kahn, 1990b) practiced by employees who feel that nothing is going to improve; they choose not to invest their energy in getting involved, speaking up, or attempting to promote change (Pinder & Harlos, 2001; van Dyne et al., 2003). The result of this type of silence is stagnation—nothing will change, and the status quo will remain intact.

Defensive or quiescent silence happens when people actively withhold information for defensive protection because they fear speaking up and anticipate an unpleasant experience (Morrison & Milliken, 2000; Pinder & Harlos, 2001; van Dyne et al., 2003). They can be reluctant to give bad news (Rosen & Tesser, 1970), feel that they are not psychologically safe (Edmondson, 1999), or sense that they lack a voice opportunity (Avery & Quiñones, 2002; Detert & Burris, 2007; Gephart et al., 2009). People who decide to execute quiescent silence are concerned about their work, have ideas, and feel invested in improving their organization. They choose to suffer in silence (Knoll & van Dick, 2013). The consequence of this type of silence is the self-protection of the person who prefers to use defensive silence.

Prosocial silence happens when not speaking up benefits the organization or others (Pinder & Harlos, 2001; van Dyne et al., 2003). There are circumstances where silence is worthwhile and rightful (Knoll & van Dick, 2013). Examples include not complaining about inconveniences at the workplace (Organ, 1988) or protecting property and private information (Knoll & van Dick, 2013). The end result of prosocial silence is protecting others from the consequences that sharing the information could have had.

However, unethical situations and acts can be covered using prosocial silence to protect the organization or people who commit wrongful acts (Umphress & Bingham, 2011). This negative aspect of prosocial silence behavior occurs to cover up errors and wrongdoing in healthcare (Gibson & Singh, 2004; Kohn et al., 1999), the government (De Maria, 2006), the police (Mollen Commission, 1994; Trautman, 2001), and educational institutions (Bogart & Stein, 1987; Miller, 1993). Eventually, unethical prosocial silence behavior will harm the organization, coworkers, patients, or clients (Knoll & van Dick, 2013).

Opportunistic silence occurs when individuals withhold information for their benefit or self-interest to confuse, misinform, or hide information (Knoll & van Dick, 2013; Williamson, 1985). Those who engage in opportunistic silence are focused on their own personal gain and accept the harming of their organization or colleagues (Knoll & van Dick, 2013).

They stay silent to avoid losing status or power and evade an extra workload (Connelly et al., 2011; Garfield, 2006). Opportunistic silence will benefit the one who uses the silence and damage those who could have benefited from the sharing of information.

The Effects of Silence Behavior

Silence behavior can devastate corporations and individuals (Wu et al., 2023). It interferes with learning and progress in organizations (Argyris & Scho¨n, 1978; Beer & Eisenstat, 2000; Dyne et al., 2003; Fast et al., 2014; Knoll et al., 2019; Knoll & van Dick, 2013; Milliken & Morrison, 2003; Morrison & Milliken, 2000; Ryan & Oestreich, 1991). Silence behavior prevents the discovery and modification of decline in an organization (Fast et al., 2014; Guo et al., 2018; Hirschman, 1970; Knoll & van Dick, 2013; Mao et al., 2019; Maqbool et al., 2019) and can for years hide violations such as psychological abuse in education institutions (Bogart & Stein, 1987), sexual harassment in the military (Klammer et al., 2001), poor clinical judgment in medicine (Gibson & Singh, 2004), and police corruption and violence (Rothwell & Baldwin, 2007).

When individuals execute silence behavior, it can create an emotional toll on them that results in feelings of shame, rage, and resentment, which negatively charge their interactions, thus decreasing productivity and creativity (Cortina & Magley, 2003; Knoll et al., 2019; Perlow & Williams, 2003). Silence behavior can cause stress (Cortina & Magley, 2003; Dedahanov et al., 2016; Dong & Chung, 2021; Morrison & Milliken, 2000), job burnout, and demoralization (Adamska & Jurek, 2017; Knoll et al., 2019; Srivastava et al., 2019). Moreover, it can decrease work innovation behavior (Fast et al., 2014; Guo et al., 2018; Maqbool et al., 2019), lower productivity, and increase wrongdoing (Dong & Chung, 2021; Milliken & Morrison, 2003). In addition, silence behavior can produce a sense of helplessness, decrease job satisfaction (Knoll et al., 2019; Milliken & Morrison, 2003; Nikolaou et al., 2011; Woo & Lee, 2018; Xu et al., 2015; Yurkadul et al., 2016), increase turnover, (Milliken & Morrison, 2003; Woo & Lee, 2018; Yurkadul et al., 2016) and result in lower employee commitment (Knoll et al., 2019; Nikolaou et al., 2011; Woo & Lee, 2018; Xu et al., 2015; Yurkadul et al., 2016). It can even cause psychological detachment and cynicism (Fleming & Spicer, 2003) and instill in workers a fear of being isolated and ignored due to a lack of support from management (Yurkadul et al., 2016; Eriguc et al., 2014; Harmanci et al., 2018). Yağar and Dumke Yağar (2023) found that silence correlated negatively with job performance (r=-0.455) and job engagement (r=-0.242) and positively with employees' intention to leave (r=0.440).

Not all silence behaviors have adverse effects. Nyberg (1993) explained that a certain amount of silence behavior is essential to promoting valued relationships among people because always telling the truth is unreal and impractical. Being silent at work can be positive when used to prevent the negative impact that speaking up may have on others. Sometimes, telling the truth can negatively affect other team members, and silence can prevent conflict (Hao et al., 2022). Prosocial silence positively affects task performance and job satisfaction when it controls other forms of silence and voice (Hao et al., 2022). For example, when a team member is responsible for an error, is personally going through a difficult time, or is having a conflict with a coworker, prosocial silence will have positive results.

Voice Behavior

Voice behavior is practiced when workers express suggestions, worries, or ideas to their company (Sherf et al., 2019; Van Dyne et al., 2003). It is a behavior that results from an intentional decision-making process after which people choose to express their ideas in their workplace to promote change (Van Dyne et al., 2003; Sherf et al., 2019). The purpose of voice behavior is to motivate others to produce change, make improvements (Morrison et al., 2014), earn achievements, and be seen as contributors to worthy results (Carver, 2006; Kakkar et al., 2016). Voice behavior is self-initiated and focused on changes and the future (Elliot, 2006; Sherf et al., 2019).

The Difference Between Speak Up and Voice Behaviors

Speak up behavior involves communicating out loud and sharing words with the team (Guttman et al., 2021; Lyndon et al., 2011).) during a meeting, when discussing cases, or simply while working in a shared physical or virtual space. Voice behavior goes further; it happens when an employee or team member speaks up about ideas, concerns, or suggestions to change or improve the organization (Van Dyne et al., 2003). Voice behavior can be seen as an evolution of speak-up behavior. The person talking has the explicit purpose of improving or changing policies at their workplace. When speaking up is executed to generate change, it becomes voice behavior.

Types of Voice Behavior

The different types of voice behavior depend on their cause, which may be disengaged, self-protective, or other-oriented behaviors based on resignation, fear, or cooperation, respectively (van Dyne et al., 2003). The types of voice behavior were identified as acquiescent, defensive or quiescent, and prosocial (van Dyne et al., 2003). The same motives are valid for silence behavior as described by van Dyne et al. (2003), with the addition of opportunistic reasons for silence (Knoll & van Dick, 2013; Williamson, 1985).

The Effects of Voice Behavior

Voice behavior is essential for an organization's success (Kao et al., 2021), performance, and functioning (Grant, 2013; Kim et al., 2010; Morrison, 2011). Moreover, it increases efficiency (LePine & Van Dyne, 1998) and improves operational functions (Morrison, 2011). In addition, voice behavior helps build a better working environment (Tullock & Hirschman, 1970), reducing turnover (McClean et al., 2013).

Relationship Between Voice and Silence Behaviors

Voice and silence behaviors are different concepts, although they may appear as extremes of a continuum (van Dyne et al., 2003; Hao et al., 2022; Knoll et al., 2016). Silence is not just keeping quiet; it has a purpose and effects. In the same fashion, voice behavior is not the same as just talking out loud. Voice is aligned with behavioral activation systems and autonomy, while silence is aligned with behavioral inhibition systems and psychological safety (Elliot, 2006; Hao et al., 2022; Sherf et al., 2021). Both voice and silence behaviors are relevant (Hao et al., 2022; Knoll & van Dick, 2013; van Dyne et al., 2003) and have their purpose. A person can simultaneously voice some ideas and suppress others (Sherf et al., 2021) during a meeting.

The absence of voice behavior does not imply silence behavior (Dyne et al., 2003; Knoll & Redman, 2016; Knoll & van Dick, 2013; Van Dyne et al., 2003). People may not know how to contribute, so they have not yet formed the internal intention to share their voice. Many authors agree that issues discouraging silence should enhance voice (Sherf et al., 2021) and that voice and silence are used to change or endure work's negative experiences (Farrell, 1983; Hirschman, 1970; Withey & Cooper, 1989).

Sherf et al. (2021) documented a negative and weak correlation between voice and silence (p= -0.15). This evidence supported the validity of Detert and Edmondson (2011) and Madrid et al. (2015), who had previously argued that there was a relationship between voice and silence. However, other investigators have found a positive correlation between voice and silence (Knoll & Redman, 2016; Wang et al., 2012). Therefore, future research is necessary to determine how voice and silence impact one another.

Reflective Analysis: Speak Up, Silence, and Voice Behaviors Scenario

An example from chapter three will be reviewed to analyze speak up, voice, and silence behaviors. This situation happened among interprofessional team members: two nurses and a physical therapist. The analysis process will begin using Kolb's Experiential Learning Perspective (Kolb, 1984; McLeod, 2024a). Then, Maslow's Hierarchy of Needs (McLeod, 2024b) will be applied to explain the behaviors.

Interprofessional Team Meeting Case

⋙ KOLB'S LEARNING PERSPECTIVE STAGES ⋘

1) **Concrete Experience**
   Jane, the clinical manager, scheduled a meeting at a round table in her office to discuss her findings regarding the accuracy of the auditors' work for the last month. Both auditors, Carla and Denise, attended. During the meeting, Jane congratulated the team for their average of 96 percent accuracy and stated that this score was a significant success. Then, Jane revealed that some errors had been discovered and discussed them in detail. The manager described the mistakes one by one.
   Upon hearing the description, Carla realized the errors described were from her cases. Carla remained silent and was visibly sweating. Denise spoke about her auditing process and made some suggestions to prevent the same errors from being made in the future. She also recommended some improvements to their auditing process that could increase their productivity as a team. Her idea was that the auditors should work remotely from their homes a few days a week to prevent frequent interruptions from administrative and clinical personnel and noise. Jane, the manager, agreed with Denise's idea. Denise continued explaining

how the interruptions made her anxious and how having a few days of uninterrupted work could improve her well-being and productivity. Jane congratulated both auditors and ended the meeting.

In the afternoon, Carla requested a private meeting with Jane to explain that she'd felt uncomfortable during the morning meeting because she'd realized she had been responsible for the mistakes. She apologized to Jane and said she would try to improve her performance. Jane told Carla that her performance was 96 percent accurate, that she should feel free to speak up during the meetings, and that discussing and correcting mistakes was part of the work. The clinical manager reiterated that her office was and would always be open for Carla to speak up about her concerns and perspectives and invited her to return to her office whenever she felt the need.

2) **Reflective Observation**

The meeting accomplished Jane's goal of analyzing the audit team's performance, but Carla felt uncomfortable after realizing that the errors discussed during the meeting were hers. She remained silent during the meeting, which showed that she did not feel psychologically safe (see analysis using Maslow's Hierarchy). Carla engaged in a defensive or quiescent silence (Morrison & Milliken, 2000; Pinder & Harlos, 2001; van Dyne et al., 2003). Jane used her speak up behavior (Guttman et al., 2021; Lyndon et al., 2011) during the meeting, explaining her findings and congratulating the team on their 96 percent compliance results. Denise used both her speak up behavior and her voice behavior (Van Dyne et al., 2003) when she reviewed her audit process (speak up), then made some suggestions to try and establish new remote-work policies (voice behavior) that would increase productivity and decrease interruptions and noise.

3) **Abstract Conceptualization**

    a. What happened? Jane, the manager, communicated the necessary information to the auditors using her speak up behavior, but the process was unpleasant for Carla, the auditor who had committed the mistakes. Carla executed a defensive or quiescent silence. Denise executed both speak up behavior when she described her auditing process and voice behavior by suggesting a new policy to increase their well-being and productivity.

      b. What went wrong? When the manager described the mistakes in detail, the auditors could deduce who'd committed the mistakes. Therefore, Carla felt uncomfortable and not psychologically safe to speak up during the meeting.

      c. What should they do next time to prevent miscommunication? The manager should not describe the errors in detail so the team members can feel psychologically safe to speak up and those who made mistakes do not feel exposed to the rest of the team.

      d. How can they improve communication within the team? In the future, discuss findings without being specific. Invite the clinicians to a communication workshop and share time in casual team-building activities to improve communication.

4) **Active Experimentation**

Next time, the manager should plan how she will discuss her findings. Discussing the results of audits in such a way that those in the meeting cannot identify who committed the mistakes may make the team members feel more comfortable and psychologically safe to speak up. In addition, Jane should take Denise's suggestions to decrease noise and interruptions during their audit process to human resources to promote policy changes.

ᔥ Maslow's Hierarchy of Needs ᔥ

In Maslow's Hierarchy of Needs, the second stage, safety needs, describes personal security, resources, health, property, and employment (Maslow, 1943; Maslow, 1954; McLeod, 2024b). Every worker values their job security so they can afford their belongings and lifestyle. The behaviors observed in the previous meeting can be analyzed according to this safety needs stage.

The clinical manager, Jane, wanted to excel in her job and facilitate a higher quality of work in the audit department. She investigated the auditors' work to calculate their precision. They obtained a 96 percent accuracy score, which wouldn't have been evidenced without her effort. She can now inform the administration of the excellent results of the audit department. In addition, she can take the official results to the quality department to demonstrate their accuracy as evidence for future accreditation visits. So, the manager's performance will establish her good status in her job with the higher levels of the organization, which aligns with the safety needs stage of Maslow's Hierarchy (Maslow, 1943; Maslow, 1954; McLeod, 2024b).

On the other hand, Carla felt uncomfortable during the meeting because the mistakes discussed were hers. She felt fear and insecurity about her job performance. Carla did not feel psychologically safe, which relates to the second stage of Maslow's Hierarchy of Needs (Maslow, 1943; Maslow, 1954; McLeod, 2024b). She decided to remain silent to avoid a negative situation. In the future, the manager must facilitate psychological safety during the team's meetings and daily work by establishing that their workplace is a safe communication space.

The other member of the audit department, Denise, wanted to excel in her job. During the meeting, she was interested in establishing her reputation as an excellent auditor when she explained her auditing process. Furthermore, she wanted to improve the productivity of their department by using her voice to make suggestions to improve their work and efficiency. Her intention relates to the second stage of Maslow's Hierarchy, safety needs (Maslow, 1943; Maslow, 1954; McLeod, 2024b). The administration and human resources would get her suggestions and probably approve her suggestions to increase their well-being and productivity. Later, if her ideas were successful, the upper level of the organization could consider moving her higher in the organization's leadership, which would be related to job safety and security needs.

Educational Activities

This section is an integral part of the learning journey throughout the book. These activities will encourage you to analyze situations and consider more profound personal experiences. Perform each activity carefully to optimize your communication skills. You can do the learning activities individually, in pairs, or with your professional team. To facilitate the activities, a template was designed to be printed by the readers. It can be used as a visual-motor aid when working on communication examples. The template is included in Appendix A.

Role-Playing: Design Scenarios

    a. Reflect on silence, voice, and speak up behaviors and think of examples based on your experiences with your team members. Who usually remains silent? Who speaks up? Who has new ideas to share using their voice behavior? Create a hypothetical meeting to practice all the behaviors as if you were in a drama class. Go back to Kolb's Experiential Learning Perspective to identify and review the behaviors. Remember the experience, reflect on it, analyze it, and practice using what you've learned.

b. Recall past experiences of ineffective communication within your team when someone was silenced during a meeting. Remember each one of the member's contributions during the experience and make notes. Reflect and discuss with a colleague what elements made the communication ineffective. Think about ways to improve communication within your team. Go back to Kolb's Experiential Learning Perspective. Remember the experience, reflect on it, analyze it, and plan for future situations.

c. Remember, reflect on, explain, and analyze examples about the benefits of effective communication and how you can make people feel comfortable during meetings in general. Go to the administrative sector of your job and explain how Medical Improv workshops, fraternization activities, and daily briefs would improve communication and trust wthin the team. Share the evidence-based results of good communication practices.

Reflection Points

- Recall and discuss examples of speak up, silence, and voice behaviors.
- What is the communication behavior that you use the most? Speak up, silence, or voice? Does it depend on who is at the meeting?
- Do you feel that some people are more receptive to your ideas than others? Do these feelings invite you to engage in speak up, silence, or voice behavior? Give examples and analyze each.
- How do you feel after remaining silent during a meeting? Think about specific examples and analyze different situations. Reflect on your experiences.
- Identify the behavior that your team members use the most. Think about examples of past meetings. Reflect on the communication experiences.
- Analyze the best way that you can improve communication within your team.

- Is the environment during your meetings at work welcoming to open communication?
- Are the upper levels of your organization's hierarchy open to communication?
- Think about ways to improve understanding within your team.

As you read other chapters, you can return to these examples to assess your learning process and see if you can solve the situations differently. In addition, you can analyze other experiences from your past using the template in Appendix A. Practice will promote deeper understanding and improve your communication skills.

Further Reading

1) **Dyne, L. V., Ang, S., & Botero, I. C.** (2003). *Conceptualizing employee silence and employee voice as multidimensional constructs.* Journal of Management Studies, 40(6), 1359–1392. https://doi.org/10.1111/1467-6486.00384.

2) **McLeod, S.** (2024a, February 2). *Kolb's learning styles and experiential learning cycle.* Simply Psychology. https://www.simplypsychology.org/learning-kolb.html.

3) **McLeod, S.** (2024b, January 24). *Maslow's Hierarchy of Needs.* Simply Psychology. https://www.simplypsychology.org/maslow.html.

4) **Wu, M., Li, W., Zhang, L., Zhang, C., & Zhou, H.** (2023). *Workplace suspicion, knowledge hiding, and silence behavior: A double-moderated mediation model of knowledge-based psychological ownership and face consciousness.* Frontiers in Psychology, 14, 982440. https://doi.org/10.3389/fpsyg.2023.982440.

5) **Sherf, E. N., Parke, M. R., & Isaakyan, S.** (2021). *Distinguishing voice and silence at work: Unique relationships with perceived impact, psychological safety, and burnout.* Academy of Management Journal, 64(1), 114–148. https://doi.org/10.5465/amj.2018.1428.

6) **Hao, L., Zhu, H., He, Y., Duan, J., Zhao, T., & Meng, H.** (2022). *When is silence golden? A meta-analysis on antecedents and outcomes of employee silence.* Journal of Business and Psychology, 37(5), 1039–1063. https://doi.org/10.1007/s10869-021-09788-.

7) **Sherf, E. N., Tangirala, S., & Venkataramani, V.** (2019). *Why managers do not seek voice from Employees: The importance of managers' personal control and long-term orientation.* Organization Science, 30(3), 447–466. https://doi.org/10.1287/orsc.2018.1273.

CHAPTER FIVE

How to Build Psychological Safety and Trust

How to Build Psychological Safety and Trust

So far, this book has explained communication, how it occurs, who is involved in the process, and why it is essential to achieving high-quality healthcare. Furthermore, we've established critical role of speak up and voice behaviors in achieving positive patient outcomes and organizational success. To speak up and promote effective collaboration, each member of a healthcare team must have trust in the others and feel psychologically safe as part of the crew. Trust, psychological safety, and speaking up are the keys to open communication. The relevance of all these elements to accomplishing effective communication is reflected in the research literature.

Experienced practitioners know that to achieve the best patient outcomes, a healthcare team must work effectively as a unit. Research evidence reinforces that such collaboration and teamwork require effective communication (Carney et al., 2019; de Assis Brito et al., 2022; Gutman et al., 2021; Nester, 2016; Pack et al., 2022; Ross et al., 2015; Royse et al., 2020). To collaborate and produce the best patient outcomes through effective communication, the members of a healthcare team should trust and respect each other and feel that their shared environment is psychologically safe. The overall purpose of this book is to support and improve team communication. The journey of writing this book has made it clear that trust is the foundation of successful communication among team members and the different levels of an organization.

Trust and Psychological Safety

Trust and psychological safety are deeply related sentiments. Psychological safety is a team construct (Edmondson, 1999; Retmulla et al., 2021) while trust is multileveled, affecting a person, their team, and their organization (Hamilton et al., 2024; Steward, 2023). **Trust** is a feeling that others will behave in your favor (CIPD, 2012; Edmondson et al., 2004). Trust can be described as feeling comfortable and safe with the people around you, confident that their actions will bring you no harm. Feeling at ease fosters creativity and innovation (Chen et al., 2021), moving an organization and its members forward. Trust is a feeling that precedes psychological safety (Hamilton et al., 2024), enabling a person to feel secure enough to share their ideas and learn from their mistakes in the workplace (Edmondson, 1999; Edmondson et al., 2004; Edmondson et al., 2016; Edmondson & Lei, 2014; Sanchez, 2019). When people have a sense of safety, they use their speak up and voice behaviors (Ge, 2020). Psychological safety sets a person into action, which is needed for effective communication and collaboration within a healthcare team.

Psychological Safety

Psychological safety refers to a person's conviction that they can talk without fear of consequences to their prestige, career, or self-image (Edmondson, 1999; Kahn, 1990a). Risky actions such as asking questions or for assistance, reporting an error, speaking about a new idea, and learning from mistakes are executed when people view their atmosphere as welcoming and safe (Edmondson, 1999; Edmondson et al., 2004; Edmondson & Lei, 2014; Sherman, 2023). Environments identified as psychologically safe facilitate the sharing of suggestions and thoughts without the fear of doing something forbidden, feeling ashamed, or being penalized for failing; psychological safety promotes learning from failures and progress (Edmondson, 1999; Edmondson et al., 2016; Edmondson & Lei, 2014; Remtulla et al., 2021; Sanchez, 2019). A person will first sense safety working with the people who form their team, and then they will feel free to share their thoughts openly. If team members change, the sense of safety may disappear.

Trust Is Essential

Trust is the key to any relationship and is aligned with quality (Berwick, 2003; O'Brien et al., 2021). Constructing trust is a process that happens over time when a team gets to work in cycles together and coordinate care for their shared patients. (Steward, 2023). Trust is experienced at different levels—as individuals, as part of a team, and in organizations (Hamilton et al., 2024; Steward, 2023). These levels can interact in complex ways. An individual may trust their own ideas and cognitive capabilities and trust certain group members but not others. At the same time, a person may trust their team but not their organization, which will impact their behavior. A person may select silence instead of voice behavior depending on who is present in a meeting and what events are happening at the organizational level.

Individuals, teams, managers, and leaders must work together to establish and maintain trust because trust is at the heart of effective communication. Trust originates from the leaders' and direct managers' behavior in organizations (CIPD, 2012). When leaders do not foster trust, they negatively impact their team's and individual team members' actions. Trust combines transparency (Hussaini & Varon, 2023; Steward, 2023) and compassion (Hussaini & Varon, 2023). When people sense safety, they can behave with full transparency and authenticity, increasing their voice behavior (Ge, 2020). This will also increase their chances of success, not only individually and for their team but also for their organization. Teams, leaders, and organizations should strive to achieve trust because it will increase their members' desire to contribute to their team's mutual success, performance, collaboration (Hamilton et al., 2024; McLean, 2005), creativity, and innovation (Chen et al., 2021).

How to Increase Trust

Increasing trust is essential for effective communication in a healthcare team (Hamilton et al., 2024). Trust reflects the team members' interactions and feelings, which are impacted by their past experiences, age, gender, education, and ethnicity (Meyer & Ward, 2008). Trust is a complex (Hamilton et al., 2024; Steward, 2023) transition (Mahon & Brookes, 2013) that impacts a team and an organization (Hamilton et al., 2024; Steward, 2023). It opens the door to the feeling of psychological safety (Hamilton et al., 2024) to promote speak up and voice behaviors (Ge, 2020). Together, team members and leaders create a group's environment (Steward, 2023). In addition, power dynamics influence a group's atmosphere (Tanco et al., 2016). Power dynamics will be the topic of chapter six.

Strategies to increase trust can be implemented at the individual, team, and organizational levels. Short meetings, known as huddles, increase trust (CIPD, 2012). Team leaders greatly influence a group's environment (CIPD, 2012; Drescher et al., 2014; King's Fund, 2014; Remtulla et al., 2012; West, 1996; West, 2021; West et al., 2003; West et al., 2020; West & Coia, 2019). Effective leadership is meant to foster and develop trust (CIPD, 2012; Drescher et al., 2014; Frith et al., 2014; Mahon, 2013; West, 2021; West & Coia, 2019) and supports learning (CIPD, 2012). Collaborative, distributive, and compassionate leadership styles increase trust and teamwork (West, 1996; West et al., 2003; Drescher et al., 2014; King's Fund, 2014).

Psychological Safety, Trust, and the Team

Psychological safety is a mental environment composed of the feelings of safety of each person as related to those around them, thus allowing them to speak up. Psychological safety is determined by team dynamics (Edmondson, 1999; Retmulla et al., 2021). It is a feeling of certainty that the crew will not reject, shame, or penalize one of its members for speaking up (Edmondson, 1999; Edmondson et al., 2016; Edmondson & Lei, 2014; Remtulla et al., 2021; Sanchez, 2019). Trust is internally sensed by the person who brings that feeling of safety into their team. Trust is experienced at many levels:

individual, team, and organization (Hamilton et al., 2024). If the rest of the team is welcoming and feels safe to a person, their environment becomes inviting and facilitates communication and collaboration within the group (Eriksen & Heimestøl, 2017; Hamilton et al., 2024). On the other hand, if the people on the team trust each other but not their organization, conversations, teamwork, and psychological safety will be negatively affected.

Psychological safety is based on mutual respect and trust (Edmondson, 1999). An act or idea that might be impossible in one group can be readily accepted by another work team due to different beliefs and consequences (Edmondson, 1999; Sherman, 2023). In healthcare teams, psychological safety is associated with increased patient safety and optimized physician involvement (Remtulla et al., 2021). For effective team synergy and outcomes, psychological safety and trust are the most important factors (Edmondson, 1999; Sherman, 2023).

Facilitators and Barriers to Psychological Safety

By studying healthcare teams' beliefs and functioning, investigators identified four barriers to psychological safety: authoritarian leadership, personality, hierarchy, and the perception of lack of knowledge (Remtulla et al., 2021). Team members working under authoritarian leaders who made decisions without consulting them felt powerless. Other healthcare team members felt that the hierarchy was forced and that their leader did not value their opinions, making them feel inferior and unsafe to use their voice behavior (Remtulla et al., 2021). In the same study, the team members who thought that they lacked knowledge had anxiety and avoided speaking up to prevent a negative experience, which has been noted by other researchers (Brinsfield, 2013; Elliot, 2006; Gutman et al., 2021; Kish-Gephart et al., 2009; Milliken & Morrison, 2003; Torralba et al., 2020).

In contrast, Remtulla et al. (2021) found the following facilitators to psychological safety: the leader, open culture, vocal personality, leader inclusiveness, support in silos, small groups, strong relationships among the members, chairing meetings, and boundary spanners. When leadership is inclusive and fosters participation, the actions of the leader will increase psychological safety, as happens in an open culture with a nonjudgmental environment, small groups, and support in silos, which are groups formed with similar people (Remtulla et al., 2021). When team members know each other well and have good relationships, it increases psychological safety too. Similarly, when using boundary spanners, persons who work as liaisons between clinical teams and administration facilitate communication between the groups and psychological safety (Remtulla et al., 2021).

Leadership and Psychological Safety

Since psychological safety and respect are outcomes of trust (Hamilton et al., 2024), all the activities and attitudes that promote trust will enable psychological safety. Leaders who want to promote trust will facilitate psychological safety (CIPD, 2012; Drescher et al., 2014; Frith et al., 2014; Mahon, 2013; Remtulla et al., 2021; West, 2021; West & Coia, 2019). Servant (Sanchez, 2019; Sinek, 2014). Collaborative, distributive, and compassionate leadership styles create psychological safety, increase trust, and promote teamwork (Drescher et al., 2014; King's Fund, 2014; West, 1996; West, 2021; West et al., 2003; West et al., 2020; West & Coia, 2019), which will ultimately improve care and patient outcomes (Steward, 2023).

Fundamental characteristics that leaders should have to foster trust within their teams are benevolence, competence, integrity (CIPD, 2012), and predictability (Dietz & Den Hartog, 2006). The leader must show genuine concern for team members (CIPD, 2012) to gain the team's trust. Fairness and honesty (Mayer et al., 2006) are equally important. Different leadership styles and distributive leadership among groups, teams, and organizations are required for different situations (CIPD, 2012; Steward, 2023) because different people and challenges require a diverse approach from their leaders.

Sinek (2014) explained that good leaders make their team feel safe, confident, and welcome. Group members feel like they belong and are motivated to create and collaborate, resulting in their ideas flourishing. The team develops camaraderie and trust, increasing motivation, innovation, energy, enthusiasm, and flavor to life (Sinek, 2014). Sherman (2023) described the steps that a leader can take to increase psychological safety: 1) Promote critical thinking by asking challenging questions, 2) Establish the importance of professional feedback in the organization's culture, including assessing and giving feedback to the leader, 3) Openly acknowledge their own mistakes, 4)Ask for help, 5) Encourage team members to challenge new ideas suggested and, 6) Promote the team's assessment and review of their previous actions, especially when things were unsuccessful.

It is important to add that ineffective and toxic leadership has countless negative results on nurses' work, outcomes, and organizational performance (Labrague et al., 2020; Roter, 2017). Future research should study toxic leadership practices and how they impact nurses' silence behavior since they are the largest professional group in healthcare (Labrague et al., 2020; Roter, 2017). Other aspects of silence behavior and its effects are included in chapter four.

Activities to Promote
Psychological Safety and Trust in Teams

To foster the speak up and voice behaviors within an interprofessional team, you need to increase their trust to generate psychological safety (Hamilton et al., 2024; Steward, 2023). People speak up when they perceive an atmosphere of psychological safety (Edmondson, 1999; Edmondson et al., 2004; Edmondson & Lei, 2014; Sherman, 2023). Evidence has demonstrated that power balance among the members of an interprofessional team ensures good communication, collaboration, coordination, and mutual responsibility (Engum & Jeffries, 2012; Hazarika, 2019; McDonald et al., 2012). Managers can promote power balance through "collaboration, an open-door policy, direct communication, education, and mentoring" (Okpala, 2021, p. 1330).

Other studies recommended workshops and activities to build the team's trust, such as relational coordination events (Guttman et al., 2021). Relational coordination events are activities outside of work so the team can share time together and get to know each other (Guttman et al., 2021). Another strategy to increase psychological safety is teaching Medical Improv (Boynton, 2022; Guttman et al., 2021; Kukora et al., 2020; Mehta et al., 2021; Watson & Fu, 2016; Watson & Fu, 2020). Medical Improv uses performance and theater improvisation techniques to improve communication and teach collaboration, naturalness, teamwork, cognition, and listening skills in the medical field (Vardell & Nelson, 2022; Watson & Fu, 2020). For a deeper understanding, look at the further reading list at the end of the chapter.

Reflective Analysis: Psychological Safety Scenario

An example used in chapters three and four will be reviewed to analyze psychological safety. This situation involved three interprofessional team members: two nurses and a physical therapist. The analysis process will begin using Kolb's Experiential Learning Perspective (Kolb, 1984; McLeod, 2024a). Then, Maslow's Hierarchy of Needs (McLeod, 2024b) will be applied to explain the behaviors.

Interprofessional Team Meeting Case

⇜ KOLB'S LEARNING PERSPECTIVE STAGES ⇝

1) **Concrete Experience**

Jane, the clinical manager, scheduled a meeting at a round table in her office to discuss her findings regarding the accuracy of the auditors' work for the last month. Both auditors, Carla and Denise, attended. During the meeting, Jane congratulated the team for their average accuracy of 96 percent and stated that this score was a significant success. Then, Jane revealed that some errors had been discovered and discussed them in detail. The manager described the mistakes one by one.

Upon hearing the description, Carla realized the errors described were from her cases. Carla remained silent and was visibly sweating. Denise spoke about her auditing process and made some suggestions to prevent the same errors from being made in the future. She also recommended some improvements to their auditing process that could increase their productivity as a team. Her idea was that the auditors should work remotely from their homes a few days a week to prevent frequent interruptions from administrative and clinical personnel and noise. Jane, the manager, agreed with Denise's idea. Denise continued explaining how the interruptions made her anxious and how having a few days of uninterrupted work could improve her well-being and productivity. Jane congratulated both auditors and ended the meeting.

In the afternoon, Carla requested a private meeting with Jane to explain that she'd felt uncomfortable during the morning meeting because she'd realized she had been responsible for the mistakes. She apologized to Jane and said she would try to improve her performance. Jane told Carla that her performance was 96 percent accurate, that she should feel free to speak up during the meetings, and that discussing and correcting mistakes was part of the work. The clinical manager reiterated that her office was and would always be open for Carla to speak up about her concerns and perspectives and invited her to return to her office whenever she felt the need.

2) **Reflective Observation**

Both Jane and Denise felt that the environment at the meeting was welcoming enough to speak up to share their ideas. They felt psychologically safe. Jane explained the audit results effectively and supported Denise's ideas. Denise reviewed her audit process and suggested establishing new remote-work policies to increase productivity and decrease interruptions and noise.

In contrast, Carla remained silent and felt uncomfortable after realizing that the errors discussed during the meeting were hers. During the first meeting, Carla did not feel psychologically safe to speak up (see analysis using Maslow's Hierarchy). Later, she asked for a private meeting with the manager to apologize for her mistakes, state her intentions to improve her work, and discuss how she'd felt during the morning meeting. When she met in private with the manager, she felt psychologically safe to speak up, which is an example of how people feel different safety levels depending on who is at the meeting.

3) **Abstract Conceptualization**

   a. What happened? Jane, the manager, and Denise could speak freely during the meeting; they felt psychologically safe. On the other hand, Carla, the auditor who had committed the mistakes, remained silent. She could not speak during the meeting and later asked for a private meeting with the manager because she did not feel psychologically safe during the initial meeting. On the other hand, she felt safe talking only to the manager during the second meeting.

   b. What went wrong? When the manager described the mistakes in detail, the auditors could deduce who had committed the mistakes. Therefore, Carla felt uncomfortable and not psychologically safe to speak up during the meeting. She was not used to getting specific feedback about her mistakes during meetings.

   c. What should they do next time to prevent miscommunication? The manager should establish that discussing mistakes is important for learning and improving outcomes in the future. This way, those who make mistakes will feel safe rather than insecure. In addition, establishing daily huddles to practice feedback and have conversations about the work, difficulties, and accomplishments within the team will gradually increase the team's psychological safety.

d. How can they improve communication within the team? In the future, discuss findings frequently so the team gets in the habit of communication and feedback. Summon the clinicians to daily communication huddles, schedule a communication workshop for all the staff, and invite the team to take part in casual team-building activities to facilitate psychological safety and trust.

4) **Active Experimentation**

Next time, the manager should try to increase trust and psychological safety within the team. She should make a plan to discuss her findings in such a way that those in the meeting cannot identify who committed the mistakes. In addition, the manager can verbalize how developing enough trust to discuss mistakes openly will improve team outcomes and promote learning, creativity, and innovation. Also, she can explain the importance of trust and psychological safety in building self-assured and happy team members who feel like they belong in their group. These actions may enable team members to feel more confident and psychologically safe.

In the future, the manager can implement daily huddles and show good leadership characteristics such as empathy, respect, camaraderie, innovation, energy, and enthusiasm to increase motivation and trust in the team. In addition, the manager should establish that their workplace is a safe communication space. She can introduce frequent professional feedback into the organization's culture to promote the team's assessment and review of their previous actions, especially when things are unsuccessful. Through practice, team members will gradually perceive feedback as a learning process to improve their outcomes as a group and not take it personally, which will increase trust and psychological safety. Moreover, the manager should convince the upper levels of the organization's hierarchy to provide workshop opportunities and fraternization activities for all the staff to increase trust and psychological safety. For other strategies, review prior sections: "Psychological Safety," "How to Increase Trust," "Activities to Promote Psychological Safety and Trust in Teams," and "Leadership and Psychological Safety."

⚜ Maslow's Hierarchy of Needs ⚜

The second stage in Maslow's Hierarchy of Needs, safety needs, describes personal security, resources, health, property, and employment (Maslow, 1943; Maslow, 1954; McLeod, 2024b). Every worker values their job security so they can afford all their needs. The actions observed in the meeting above can be analyzed according to this safety needs stage. Review Figure 3 (pg. 16) depicting Maslow's Hierarchy of Needs.

Every team member wants to excel at their job to demonstrate the quality of their performance and fulfill their safety needs. From the manager's perspective, all the team members excelled at their jobs, which was established during the meeting. They got excellent results at the audit, and the manager performed her assessment successfully. Their performance proved their excellence to the higher levels of the organization, thus providing job security and fulfilling the safety needs stage of Maslow's Hierarchy (Maslow, 1943; Maslow, 1954; McLeod, 2024b).

At the same time, Carla felt uncomfortable during the meeting because the mistakes discussed were hers. She felt fear and insecurity about her job performance. Carla did not feel psychologically safe, which relates to the second stage of Maslow's Hierarchy of Needs (Maslow, 1943; Maslow, 1954; McLeod, 2024b). She decided to remain silent to avoid a negative situation. On the other hand, at the second meeting with the manager, Carla felt safe to speak up. Carla felt safe with the manager but not with the team when her peer was present. Increasing psychological safety and trust will make the team feel their safety needs are fulfilled.

Educational Activities

This section is an essential part of the learning journey throughout the book. These activities will encourage you to analyze situations and consider more profound personal experiences. Perform each activity carefully to optimize your communication skills. You can do the learning activities individually, in pairs, or with your professional team. To facilitate the activities, a template was designed to be printed by the readers. It can be used as a visual-motor aid when working on communication examples. The template is included in Appendix A.

Role-Playing: Design Scenarios

      a. Reflect on psychological safety and trust and think of examples based on your experiences with your team members. What increases your trust? What makes you feel that you cannot speak up? Who do you trust? Do you trust all the people on your team? Do you trust the organization that you work for? Create a hypothetical meeting to practice behaviors that improve trust and safety. Go back to Kolb's Experiential Learning Perspective to identify and review the behaviors. Remember the experience, reflect on it, analyze it, and practice using what you've learned.

b. Recall a past experiences when someone was silenced during a meeting, causing a lack of psychological safety within your team. Remember each team member's contributions during the experience and make notes. Reflect and discuss with a colleague what elements made the communication ineffective. Think about ways to improve communication, psychological safety, and trust within your team. Go back to Kolb's Experiential Learning Perspective. Remember the experience, reflect, analyze, and plan for future situations.

c. Remember, reflect on, explain, and analyze examples about the benefits of effective communication and how you can make people feel comfortable during meetings in general. Go to the administrative sector of your job and explain how Medical Improv workshops, fraternization activities, and daily briefs or huddles would improve communication and trust within the team. Share the evidence-based results of good communication practices.

Reflection Points

➢ Remember how you sense trust in a team member. Define trust and give examples of it within a healthcare team.

➢ Describe psychological safety and recall situations where you have felt safe to speak up. Give examples.

➢ What is the communication behavior that you use the most? Speak up, silence, or voice? Does it depend upon who is at the meeting?

➢ Do you feel that some people are more receptive to your ideas than others? Do these feelings invite you to use speak up, silence, or voice behavior? Give examples and analyze each one.

➢ Consider how to increase trust within your healthcare professional team.

- Describe and analyze how a leader can contribute to trust and psychological safety for a team.
- Remember the teams you have worked with and describe the environment you sensed when working with them. Was the leadership effective? Did it increase trust and psychological safety?
- How do you feel after remaining silent during a meeting? Why do you sometimes decide not to speak up? Think about specific examples and analyze them. Reflect on your experiences.
- How do you feel after using your voice behavior? What makes you choose to express your new ideas? How does your level of trust in your team contribute? Think about specific examples and analyze them. Reflect on your experiences.
- Identify the communication behavior that your team members use the most. Think about examples of past meetings. Reflect on the communication experiences.
- Think of the best way that you can improve communication within your team.
- Is the environment during your meetings at work welcoming to open communication?
- Are the upper levels of your organization's hierarchy open to communication?
- Think about ways to improve understanding and compatibility within your team.

As you read other chapters, you can return to these examples to assess your learning process and see if you can solve the situations differently. In addition, you can analyze other experiences from your past using the template in Appendix A. Practice will promote deeper understanding and improve your communication skills.

Further Reading

1) Edmondson, A. C., Higgins, M., Singer, S., & Weiner, J. (2016). *Understanding psychological safety in health care and education organizations: A comparative perspective. research in human development, 13(1), 65–83.* https://doi.org/10.1080/15427609.2016.1141280.

2) Edmondson, A. C., Kramer, R. M., & Cook, K. S. (2004). *Psychological safety, trust, and learning in organizations: A group-level lens.* Trust and distrust in organizations: Dilemmas and Approaches, 12(2004), 239-272.

3) Edmondson, A. C., & Lei, Z. (2014). *Psychological safety: The history, renais-*

sance, and future of an interpersonal construct. Annual Review of Organizational Psychology and Organizational Behavior, 1 (1), 23–43. https://doi.org/10.1146/annurev-orgpsych-031413-091305.

4) Steward, E. (2023). *Interprofessional team trust in maternity services: a service evaluation.* British Journal of Midwifery, 31(3), 126–132. https://doi.org/10.12968/bjom.2023.31.3.126.

5) Hussaini, N., & Varon, J. (2023). *Fostering trust in critical care medicine: A comprehensive analysis of patient-provider relationships.* Critical Care & Shock, 26(6). ISSN 1410-7767.

6) Hamilton, A. L., Layden, E. A., Storrar, N., Skinner, J., Harden, J., & Wood, M. (2024). *Definition, measurement, precursors, and outcomes of trust within health care teams: A scoping review.* Academic Medicine, 99(1), 106–117. https://doi.org/10.1097/acm.0000000000005320.

7) Sinek, S. (2014, March). *Why good leaders make you feel safe.* [Video] TED Conferences. https://video.search.yahoo.com/search/video?fr=mcafee&p=why+good+leaders+make+you+feel+safe+from+ted+2014+by+simon+sinek+on+march+2014&type=E210US1500G0#id=1&vid=4e8467464e8815a85f7adcfdc4f9cc2e&action=click.

8) McLeod, S. (2024a, February 2). *Kolb's learning styles and experiential learning cycle.* Simply Psychology. https://www.simplypsychology.org/learning-kolb.html.

9) McLeod, S. (2024b, January 24). Maslow's Hierarchy of Needs. Simply Psychology. https://www.simplypsychology.org/maslow.html.

10) Boynton, B. [Beth Boynton]. (2022, February 16). *Introduction to Medical Improv for Leaders – Reinventing Communication & Culture in Healthcare.* [Video] YouTube. https://www.youtube.com/watch?v=u25fw_h4Zvg.

11) Kukora, S. K., Batell, B., Umoren, R., Gray, M. M., Ravi, N., Thompson, C., & Zikmund-Fisher, B. J. (2020). *Hilariously bad news: Medical Improv as a novel approach to teach communication skills for bad news disclosure.* Academic Pediatrics, 20(6), 879–881. https://doi.org/10.1016/j.acap.2020.05.003.

12) Mehta, A., Fu, B., Chou, E., Mitchell, S., & Fessell, D. (2021). *Improv: Transforming physicians and medicine.* Medical Science Educator, 31(1), 263–266. https://doi.org/10.1007/s40670-020-01174-x.

13) Watson, K., & Fu, B. (2016). *Medical Improv: A novel approach to teaching communication and professionalism skills.* Annals of Internal Medicine, 165(8), 591. https://doi.org/10.7326/m15-2239.

14) Watson, K. & Fu, B. (2020). *What is Medical Improv?* https://www.medicalimprov.org/about.

15) Vardell, E., & Nelson, S. B. (2022). *Teaching reference interview skills with Improv.* Journal of Education for Library and Information Science, 63(1), 38–56. https://doi.org/10.3138/jelis-2020-0098.

CHAPTER SIX

Power Dynamics and Communication

Power Dynamics and Communication

Power balance among team members is one of the aspects that determines a team's success (Crowe et al., 2017; McDonald et al., 2012; Okpala, 2021; Rogers et al., 2024). Evidence has demonstrated that power balance among the members of an interprofessional team ensures good communication, collaboration, coordination, and mutual responsibility (Engum & Jeffries, 2012; Hazarika, 2019; McDonald et al., 2012). Effective communication, teamwork, and power balance will facilitate a team's ability to optimize patient care. Factors that affect power dynamics and different strategies to promote power balance will be discussed in this chapter.

Power and Power Imbalance

Power is the control and possession of resources to determine the strategies to engage the healthcare team in their work and goals (Engum & Jeffries, 2012). Power is like having the keys that open the door to the means and opportunities for success. The keys should be shared among team members, giving them turns depending on each person's experiences and expertise to create a power balance. For example, if a patient's primary needs are related to aphasia and decreased mobility, the co-leaders on that specific case should be the speech language pathologist and the physical therapist. They have the required expertise in the most relevant areas of the plan of care. The active participation of the rest of the interprofessional team is required to optimize patient outcomes, add different perspectives, and identify patients' needs according to their experience and capabilities. Effective communication and collaboration happen when all team members share power, which results in effective teamwork, collaboration, and communication essential to optimizing patient outcomes.

 Power imbalance is the dominance of one professional group; this can be the product of differences among team members, such as their backgrounds, education, and abilities, as well as compatibility issues (Hart, 2015). These differences among team members and miscommunication will affect the team's outcomes (Hart, 2015). Power imbalance happens when dominated groups are eliminated from the decision-making processes; as a result, their concerns cannot be addressed (Lloyd et al., 2011; Nimmon & Stenfors-Hayes, 2016). Individuals who feel power imbalances describe them as negative feelings of self-preservation, misunderstanding, and manipulation created by those with power (Kovič & McMahon, 2023). Power imbalance must be identified and addressed to promote optimal outcomes (Okpala,

2021; Rogers et al., 2024). Not sharing the power among team members will affect patient outcomes because every health professional has an essential role on the team based on where they excel. Interprofessional teamwork is crucial for clinical success, and power imbalance interferes with interprofessional collaboration.

Hierarchies and Dominance

Although more non-physician health professionals have developed prominence in science, physicians remain at the top of the interprofessional hierarchies (Noyes, 2022). Investigations demonstrate that health organizations are frequently structured hierarchically, with physicians at the top of their staff (Aase, 2016; Tang et al., 2013). Given these hierarchical structures, one needs to understand the possibility of dominance, in which one group directs, regulates, and overpowers others (Hansson et al.,2010; Lee et al., 2022; Luetsch & Scuderi, 2020); they own the power. Research has shown that interprofessional teamwork ensures optimal outcomes (Carney et al., 2019; de Assis Brito et al., 2022; Gutman et al., 2021; Nester, 2016; Pack et al., 2022; Ross et al., 2015; Royse et al., 2020) whereas dominance and hierarchy may compromise teamwork (Noyes, 2022) and challenge collaborative health models (Findyartini et al., 2019). To provide effective services to patients, there is an imperative need for teamwork (Nester, 2016) and power balance, which mitigate hierarchies and dominance.

Leadership to Promote Power Balance

Effective leadership that strives to promote power balance can mitigate the dangers of power imbalance and dominance. Effective leaders must promote shared collaboration and decision-making (Weberg, 2012), the opposite of dominance, power, and traditional hierarchy. Leaders should work to ensure power balance so their team can provide effective health services (Okpala, 2021). Many researchers have demonstrated that leaders of healthcare teams are responsible for creating the work and organizational philosophy that will inform how individuals relate to each other as part of the team (Taplin et al., 2013). Leaders must use strategies to promote effective communication, proper role allocation, trust, respect, and the enhancement of team attitudes and skills (Okpala, 2021). The strategies to promote power balance within a team include using a collaborative approach, direct communication, an open-door policy, mentoring, and education (Okpala, 2021). In addition, the leader should use a merit-based approach when appointing guidance roles to team members (Okpala, 2021).

A leader having a genuine disposition and being willing to share power is essential and empowers team members (Kovič & McMahon, 2023). Power sharing happens when leaders show warmth and empathy, are transparent about their battles, and trust their team members' abilities (De Stefano et al., 2017). Individuals feel valued, safe, supported, and entrusted when their supervisors respect them as clinicians (Kovič & McMahon, 2023). Deep and productive alliances can develop when leaders and team members are willing to trust in and engage with each other (Kovič & McMahon, 2023). People find that getting to know their team and having informal contact with the other team members helps them develop a stronger connection with each other as well as trust (Guttman et al., 2021; Kovič & McMahon, 2023), which lessens power imbalance (Kovič & McMahon, 2023). When a team feels trusted and enabled by their leader, the power dynamic is experienced as accepting rather than restraining (Kovič & McMahon, 2023). This feeling of empowerment and safety will promote effective communication and teamwork.

Communication Relevance and Power Imbalance

Health professionals, team members, leaders, and management must consider the relationship between communication and power imbalance. Understanding power dynamics, making the intentional effort to improve communication, and flattening the hierarchies within a healthcare team and an organization will produce good teamwork, collaboration, and success. Researchers have found that effective collaboration within a team requires good communication, which is promoted by power balance (Engum & Jeffries, 2012; Hazarika, 2019; McDonald et al., 2012). Communication issues can be resolved by practicing direct communication, collaboration, and an open-door approaches; at the same time, those strategies can improve power balance within a healthcare team (Okpala, 2021).

Silence Behavior and Power Balance

In the chapter about speak up, voice, and silence behaviors, we learned that people must speak up to participate in their team's decision-making process. Power imbalance can be the product of differences among team members and interfere with effective communication and teamwork (Hart, 2015). A power imbalance can silence those who feel negative feelings of manipulation and are misunderstood by those who dominate (Kovič & McMahon, 2023). Every team must work on power balance to promote speak up and voice behaviors among their teammates.

Factors that Influence Power Dynamics

It is essential to identify the factors that affect power dynamics to understand and optimize teamwork (Okpala, 2021; Rogers et al., 2024). The five groups of factors that affect power dynamics in healthcare teams identified by Okpala (2021) are:

- Team-related
- Related to role allocation
- Communication and team-related factors
- Level of trust and respect
- Related to the person

Team-Related Factors

One of the team-related factors that affects power balance is the implementation of dominance in the medical hierarchy. This occurs when team members feel like they cannot challenge a physician's ideas because they are intimidated (Green et al., 2017). This is a circumstance in which the leadership structure obeys classic medical dominance. The abilities or relative experiences of the different team members are not respected. In this case, if a group member is a physician, the leadership position is assigned only because of their degree, and the rest of the team members' ideas may not be valued. Another team-related factor is the limited or uneven provision of space and time to a group, a situation in which there is no place or time given for the group to perform duties or provide their perspectives (Gum et al., 2012; Johnson, 2016). A group that cannot meet to work or discuss their take on events cannot share the power.

Role Allocation Factors

Role allocation factors refer to circumstances in which there is a lack of recognition and confidence in the skills and expertise of others and a blurry delineation of team members' roles (Okpala, 2021). When team members do not understand each team member's role, responsibilities, and boundaries, the decision-making process and collaboration within the team are affected negatively (McDonald et al., 2012). When this happens, power dynamics are affected (Okpala, 2021). Each person should understand and respect their own role and the expertise of others to optimize communication, group dynamics, and patient outcomes.

Communication and Team-Related Factors

Communication and team-related factors refer to the tone of communication, responsiveness, and receptivity within the team (Okpala, 2021). It is important to note that some people use communication strategies such as withholding communication to keep their power and obliterate other team members (Okpala, 2021). When communication within the team is ineffective, it affects group dynamics, promoting power imbalance. To optimize teamwork and collaboration, thus facilitating a strong group dynamic, team members should be open, approachable, and receptive to communication coming from everyone..

Trust and Respect

High levels of **trust and respect** will affect power dynamics positively (Okpala, 2021). As explained in chapter five, mutual respect and trust are the foundation of collaboration, teamwork, and effective communication. When people have hidden agendas and damaging attitudes toward each other, it will directly affect communication effectiveness and produce a power imbalance. Power imbalance must be identified and addressed because they interfere with patient outcomes (Okpala, 2021; Rogers et al., 2024). Increasing trust and respect will improve communication and power balance within the team.

Factors Related to the Individual

Factors related to the individual are the attitudes, skills, and expertise each team member contributes to the group (Okpala, 2021). Every person has characteristics, experiences, and knowledge that will benefit the team when a positive attitude of communication and collaboration occurs. When each team member knows their roles, responsibilities, and limits, their decision-making process will be effective (McDonald et al., 2021). If, on the other hand, conflicts, secrets, gossip, and rivalries prevail, power balance and teamwork will be hindered.

Strategies to Facilitate Power Balance

Producing power balance is crucial to optimize communication, collaboration, and teamwork (Okpala, 2021; Rogers et al., 2024). The six strategies to promote power dynamics found by Okpala (2021) are:

- An open-door policy
- A collaborative approach
- Education
- Mentoring
- Direct communication
- A merit-based approach to assigning leadership roles

Open-Door Policy

It is important to understand that an **open-door policy** does not only mean leaving the door of the clinical manager's office physically open. It refers to a leader's positive attitude, receptivity, and efforts to make the team feel heard, valued, trusted, and welcomed. It is a common experience for team members to hear managers and members of the upper hierarchy in organizations repeatedly say that they have an open-door policy when they frequently demonstrate to the staff that their ideas are not valued and will not bring about change and progress. Truly opening the door means proving a leader's unbiased honesty and trustfulness with positive actions, changes, and outcomes for their teams, positively impacting the organization over time.

Collaborative Approach

A **collaborative approach** happens when all team members can speak up and voice their new ideas to produce change. Health professionals bring different perspectives, knowledge, and traditions to the table to solve healthcare problems (Willumsen, 2016). Interprofessional collaboration happens when team members work together to facilitate and produce a positive effect on their patients' health using their varied interactions, negotiations, contributions, and expertise (Reeves et al., 2017; Willumsen, 2016). In addition, if a leader supports their team effectively, the team members will feel psychologically safe and understand that the power is balanced among them, thus promoting teamwork and collaboration.

Direct Communication

Another strategy to promote power balance is using **direct communication**. Examples include face-to-face and telephone conversations that allow team members to feel unity and partnership (Okpala, 2021). Eye contact and active listening are essential. Collaboration and cohesion can be enhanced when the proper tone is used (Mueller et al., 2014; Okpala, 2017). The proper tone is practiced when verbal and nonverbal communication within the team are aligned and perceived as positive, genuine, aligned, and welcoming. Direct communication is the best way to communicate if the people involved are engaged and receptive.

Education

Education moves a team forward toward power balance (Okpala, 2021). A team should be educated and receive updated information about their professionalism, their specific roles, and the requirements for the organization's accreditations relevant to them as health services providers. This way, the whole team forge a true power balance with no hidden information. Each team member will understand their value and expertise regarding their experience within the group. By the same token, each team member will understand the value of other team members, moving with the organization toward teamwork, collaboration, and success.

Mentoring

Mentoring promotes power balance in the healthcare team (Okpala, 2021). Appointing someone as a mentor who understands the group dynamics and the organizational culture is very helpful in accomplishing an effective intake process when a new team member arrives. New members may feel intimidated by the unfamiliar working environment. Having a mentor will facilitate their progress as they settle in. This way, the new members will learn the characteristics and roles of the team and the relevance of their own work as a part of the team. The integration process will be smoother and more enjoyable because they will feel supported by the mentor along the way, promoting a welcoming environment within the group.

Merit-Based Approach to Assigning Leadership Roles

A **merit-based approach to assigning leadership roles** within the team will facilitate power balance (Okpala, 2021). The leader should assign roles according to team members' experience and not the traditional medical hierarchy. This way, team members will understand that everyone can move into leadership positions according to their performance and experience. Classical traditions in which physicians assume leadership roles just because of their degrees are counterproductive to teamwork and collaboration (Findyartini et al., 2019). Merit-based leadership assignments will improve power balance (Okpala, 2021), allowing team members to trust that career growth is possible for anyone.

Activities to Improve Group Dynamics

Narasimhan (2023) suggested different activities to improve group dynamics. First, teams should understand that communication is the main process occurring during their meetings (Narasimhan, 2023) and prioritize its relevance. A good practice is for team leaders to identify after each meeting which behaviors either encouraged or impeded open communication by making a list of processes and taking a poll to assess the performance of each (Narasimhan, 2023). Then, the team can straightforwardly analyze and review the communication processes that occurred during their meeting with the purpose of understanding and improving their communication as a team (Narasimhan, 2023). This conscious assessment of their communication methods will produce self-awareness within the team and improve their meetings' effectiveness..

Similarly, the board of directors and other higher-ups in an institution should create a positive organizational culture to promote effective communication (Narasimhan, 2023). By facilitating a power balance, they will improve communication within the team and raise their chances of success. They should create a positive communication environment of psychological safety in which the staff will feel free to express their ideas and concerns without fear of retaliation (Narasimhan, 2023). To accomplish this task, the leaders should consistently remind each staff member of their value, expressing empathy and honest support. The leader's actions should be aligned with the whole group's ideals to increase trust between the team and the organization. If misalignments and contradictions happen frequently, trust levels will decline.

An equally important part of this process should be the identification of disruptive and dominant figures within the team, especially when they are part of the upper hierarchy of the organization (Narasimhan, 2023). Board members should arrange direct communication interventions with the persons identified to promote their self-awareness and self-regulation. These tactics will make them aware of the adverse effects of their communication habits and help them adjust and improve their behavior during meetings (Narasimhan, 2023). This active analysis of the communication process among the team is accomplished by doing surveys, polls, and visual diagrams about their communication lines after their meeting, which can make the team members aware of their behaviors (Narasimhan, 2023). Another way of improving group dynamics within the team is to practice communication in formal and informal activities (Guttman et al., 2021; Narasimhan, 2023).

Reflective Analysis: Dominance Hierarchy and Power Balance Scenario

A description of a team meeting will be used to analyze dominance, hierarchy, and power balance. This situation happened between interprofessional team members (two nurses, one occupational therapist, and one speech language pathologist), the clinical manager (Margot, a physical therapist), and the president and vice president (both physicians) of the board of directors. The analysis process will begin using Kolb's Experiential Learning Perspective (Kolb, 1984; McLeod, 2024a). Then, Maslow's Hierarchy of Needs (McLeod, 2024b) will be applied to explain the behaviors.

Meeting with Interprofessional Team and Board of Directors

≫ KOLB'S LEARNING PERSPECTIVE STAGES ≪

1) **Concrete Experience**
   The company's owner and president of the board of directors for three months, Jackeline, had just graduated from the school of medicine and inherited her position in the company from her parents, who had retired. Her cousin José, also a young graduate physician, was appointed by her to be the vice president of the board. Neither of them had any previous experience or contact with the institution. During the last five years, the interprofessional team had been guiding the agency successfully, working with the previous board of directors and scheduling meetings every two weeks. Jackeline summoned the attendees for a meeting without explaining the situation she wanted to discuss.

   The members of the interprofessional team who were invited were surprised and had to change their schedules and cancel previous appointments to attend the meeting. The interprofessional team members were worried about the short notice of the meeting and its content. When they arrived, Jackeline looked somber and disappointed. She explained that she had decided to call an emergency meeting to discuss a new finding she had become aware of through a confidential source. Jackeline said that the last accreditation report had included a recommendation to change the education process for patients, and a staff member had informed her about instances of noncompliance that had been found in many clinical records since the start of the year.

The clinical manager, Margot, was unaware of the situation. She met with her team weekly to assess concerns and followed up on all problems they had identified, including issues with clinical documentation and education on how to fix them. When Margot started to explain her perspective on the situation and how the team had handled this clinical record issue successfully in the past, Jackeline responded that she was not interested in previous experiences and would implement her own ideas. The rest of the interprofessional team felt Jackeline was being disrespectful to Margot. Claudia, a nurse, and the other team members tried to speak up, but Jackeline said the purpose of the meeting was informative, then imparted instructions about what would happen next. José, the vice president, felt intimidated by and inexperienced compared to the people at the meeting; he decided not to speak up.

After the meeting, the team went to the clinical manager's office to complain about Jackeline's decision-making process. Some said they were thinking about quitting if this type of leadership continued. They also asked the clinical manager to name the staff member who spoke about the record problem with the board president without informing the team first.

2) **Reflective Observation**

The meeting accomplished Jackeline's three goals: exposing an issue with clinical records, demonstrating that she had a secret ally on the team, and explaining how the decisions would be made under her leadership. She showed the team that she would be their boss and that the team's five years of successful experience working together, along with their input, did not matter to her. The clinical manager and the rest of the healthcare team could not express their ideas to solve the problem because Jackeline silenced them using her dominant authority. The team was used to the successful teamwork and power balance they experienced with the previous board of directors.

Both the president and vice president of the board were appointed because they were family members of former board members and young physicians. They had no previous experience working with the organization. This decision reflected dominance and compliance with the traditional hierarchy. This created a power imbalance by centralizing power in the president of the board, which obliterated the rest of the team's voice behavior.

3) **Abstract Conceptualization**

    a. What happened? Jackeline, the president of the board of directors, held a surprise meeting to inform the team about some decisions that she had made unilaterally. The clinical manager tried to speak up but was silenced by the president, who was not interested in the previous experiences of the team. Other team members felt discouraged and could not speak up. The vice president felt intimidated and remained silent.

    b. What went wrong? The board president displayed a dictatorial-destructive leadership style; she had her own ideas and was not interested in teamwork. She gave orders and expected the team to follow without discussion or analysis. The team was disappointed in Jackeline's leadership style, and many thought about quitting and searching for new jobs.

    c. What should they do next time to prevent miscommunication? The president should be educated about the importance of effective communication and teamwork. Working with the team rather than giving them orders will promote optimal patient outcomes, communication, trust, power balance, and success not only for the team but for the organization. Maybe Margot, the clinical manager, could ask for a private meeting with the president to discuss these topics.

    d. How could communication among team members be improved? In the future, invite the president and the board members to a communication workshop and casual team-building activities to improve the communication and power balance between the team and the board of directors.

4) **Active Experimentation**

Next time, the president should plan ahead and communicate privately with the clinical manager before holding a team meeting so she can establish a good working relationship with the clinical manager and build trust with the larger team. Jackeline should work to understand the team's effective collaboration and teamwork for the last five years when they worked with the previous board of directors.

⪢ Maslow's Hierarchy of Needs ⪡

In Maslow's Hierarchy of Needs, the third and fourth stages explain love and belonging—the need for connection in a group—and esteem—the need for self-esteem, recognition, and freedom (Maslow, 1943; Maslow, 1954; McLeod, 2024b). In the meeting described above, the team, which had been working successfully for five years felt that the new president had failed to fulfill their needs of love, belonging, and esteem. The president did not respect their clinical manager and ended their positive experience of five years of continuous and successful work. Another level of the hierarchy that could be involved in this example is self-actualization because team members perceived that their professional development would be impossible under destructive leadership. Their feelings were so strong that they expressed their desire to quit to their clinical manager after the meeting. Review Figure 3 (pg. 16) depicting Haslow's Hierarchy of Needs.

Educational Activities

This section is an integral part of the learning journey throughout the book. These activities will encourage you to analyze situations and consider more profound personal experiences. Perform each activity carefully to optimize your communication skills. You can do the learning activities individually, in pairs, or with your professional team. To facilitate the activities, a template was designed to be printed by the readers. It can be used as a visual-motor aid when working on communication examples. The template is included in Appendix A.

Role-Playing: Design Scenarios

a. Reflect on power balance, dominance, and traditional hierarchies and think of examples based on your experiences. Who has the power? Is there a group that dominates? Describe a traditional hierarchy. Who shares new ideas in the group using their voice behavior? Who remains silent? Is there a member of the team who interferes with the communication? Create a hypothetical meeting to practice all the behaviors as if you were in a drama class. Go back to Kolb's Experiential Learning Theory to identify and review the behaviors. Remember the experience, reflect on it, analyze it, and practice using what you've learned.

b. Recall past experiences of ineffective communication within your team when someone was silenced during a meeting. Remember each member's contributions during the experience and make notes. Reflect and discuss with a colleague what elements made the communication ineffective. Think about ways to improve communication within your team. Go back to Kolb's Experiential Learning Theory. Remember the experience, reflect on it, analyze it, and plan for future situations.

c. Remember, reflect on, explain, and analyze examples about the benefits of effective communication and how you can make people feel comfortable during meetings in general. Go to the administrative sector of your job and explain how an open-door policy, a collaborative approach, direct communication, education, and mentoring improve power balance. Then, explain how sending out polls, surveys, and visual diagrams regarding the team's communication processes after a meeting will improve group dynamics. In addition, explain how Medical Improv workshops, fraternization activities, and daily briefs would improve communication and trust within the team. Share the evidence-based results of good communication practices.

Reflection Points

- Recall and discuss examples of power, dominance, and traditional hierarchy.
- Have you experienced a power imbalance? How did you feel about it? Recall the situation and analyze it.
- Think about your interprofessional team. Is the power balanced among the members?
- Consider if there is a power imbalance within your team. Do team members' behaviors change depending on who is at the meeting?
- Is there a powerful person who interferes with the communication processes during your team meetings? What are the behaviors?

- Do people intimidate you at your team or board of directors meetings? Do you feel that you cannot speak up? How does that make you feel?
- Do you feel that some people are more receptive to your ideas than others? Do these feelings invite you to use speak up, silence, or voice behavior? Give examples and analyze each one.
- How do you feel after remaining silent during a meeting? Think about specific examples and analyze each situation. Reflect on your experiences.
- Do you trust your team? Do you trust the upper levels of your organization's hierarchy? Do they display productive leadership patterns?
- Identify the communication behavior that your team members use the most. Think about examples of past meetings. Reflect on the communication experiences.
- Analyze the best way to improve communication within your team.
- Does the environment of your work meetings welcome open communication?
- Is the upper hierarchy of your organization open to communication? Explain.
- Think about ways to improve understanding team members to avoid an inadvertent power imbalance.
- Reflect on how power imbalance affects your teamwork and the organization. Is there progress or stagnation?
- Think about the strategies to promote power balance and give examples. Remember, these are an open-door policy, a collaborative approach, education, mentoring, direct communication, and a merit-based approach to assigning leadership roles.

As you read other chapters, you can return to these examples to assess your learning process and see if you can solve the situations differently. In addition, you can recall other experiences from your past using the template in Appendix A. Practice will promote deeper understanding and improve your communication skills.

Further Reading

1) **Okpala, P.** (2021). *Addressing power dynamics in interprofessional health care teams.* International Journal of Healthcare Management, 14(4), 1326–

1332. https://doi.org/10.1080/20479700.2020.1758894.

2) Rogers, L., Hughes Spence, S., Aivalli, P., De Brún, A., & McAuliffe, E. (2024). *A systematic review critically appraising quantitative survey measures assessing power dynamics among multidisciplinary teams in acute care settings.* Journal of Interprofessional Care, 38(1), 156–171. https://doi.org/10.1080/13561820.2023.2168632.

3) Okpala, P. (2017). *Harnessing the power of collaborative leadership in the management of chronic health conditions. International Journal of Healthcare Management, 12(4), 302–307.* https://doi.org/10.1080/20479700.2017.1414109.

4) Hart, C. (2015). *The elephant in the room: Nursing and nursing power on an interprofessional team.* The Journal of Continuing Education in Nursing, 46(8), 349–355. https://doi.org/10.3928/00220124-20150721-15.

5) Narasimhan, A. (2023). *Raising vital voices in the boardroom: Group dynamics can stop members Speaking out, so how do we empower them? By Anand Narasimhan.* Financial Times, 21-23. https://www.ft.com/content/99e17420-2628-43ba-b6f4-e9cc25d48e9b.

6) Nester, J. (2016). *The importance of interprofessional practice and education in the era of accountable care.* North Carolina Medical Journal, 77(2), 128–132. https://doi.org/10.18043/ncm.77.2.128.

7) Kovič, D., & McMahon, A. (2023). *Building trust: supervisees' experience of power dynamics in transdisciplinary workplace supervision. Journal of Social Work Practice, 37(4), 403–417.* https://doi.org/10.1080/02650533.2022.216249.

8) Guttman, O. T., Lazzara, E. H., Keebler, J. R., Webster, K. L., Gisick, L. M., & Baker, A. L. (2021). *Dissecting communication barriers in healthcare: A path to enhancing communication resiliency, reliability, and patient safety.* Journal of Patient Safety, 17(8), e1465-e1471. https://doi.org/10.1097/pts.0000000000000541.

CHAPTER SEVEN

———○———

Attitudes and Perceptions of Communication and Collaboration

Attitudes and Perceptions
of Communication and Collaboration

The importance of effective communication within a healthcare team has been thoroughly explained in past chapters. Effective communication and collaboration are deeply related. The team members interested in optimizing their teamwork will want to improve their communication skills. Communication and teamwork support effective exchanges with patients, communities, families, and health professionals (Tolle et al., 2019). Breakdowns in collaboration within a team negatively impact the work environment, patient care and outcomes, which increase healthcare costs (Barnard et al., 2020). In this chapter, we will discuss how attitudes and perceptions impact communication and collaboration and how to promote positive attitudes and perceptions in the workplace.

Collaboration, communication, and cooperation are essential for interprofessional teams and organizations (Castañer & Oliveira, 2020; Wang et al., 2022; WHO, 2010). There should be conscious and organized efforts to promote positivity among clinicians regarding effective teamwork and collaborative interactions. This positivity will support optimized team outcomes and make life easier for each individual. Discovering how to produce and reinforce positive attitudes toward, perceptions of, and experiences with communication and collaboration will improve the daily work process for every team member (Ansa et al., 2020).

It is known that positive attitudes and perceptions about collaboration and communication facilitate teamwork (Tolle et al., 2019; WHO, 2010). Typically, healthcare professionals become a part of a team when they start a job. Every member must adapt to the team's and organization's policies and procedures to reach common goals. Each person brings their unique input, positive or negative, to the team. Negative attitudes and perceptions interfere with collaboration and communication processes within the team. Creating positive perceptions of and attitudes toward communication and collaboration will facilitate teamwork.

Perceptions

Understanding perceptions is fundamental to creating positive perceptions of communication and collaboration. People receive information from their environment through their senses by hearing, seeing, smelling, tasting, and touching; that sensory information is transmitted to their brains (Cherry, 2023b). These sensory inputs are transformed into perceptions of sounds, tastes, touches, and sights (Cherry,2023b). For example, health professionals may hear a colleague's voice, taste their lunch, examine or touch their patients, and see MRIs and X-rays. In summary, individuals receive information from their environment to form their unique **sensory perceptive experience**. Psychology theorists explain the process of the formation of perceptions in different ways (Cherry, 2023b). Some say that perceptions come directly from the input of the environment and reflect an objective experience (Gibson, 1966, 1972). Others argue that perceptions come from the expectations and previous knowledge of the individual, which is added to the stimulus itself (Cherry, 2023b; Gregory, 1970, 1974).

Learning involves perceptions. Perceptions lead to attitudes, and attitudes then influence future perceptions. It is a life cycle; people perceive their environment, then construct their attitudes as life goes on. If perceptions are influenced by the previous knowledge and understanding of the perceiver (Cherry, 2023b; Gregory, 1970, 1974), then creating or changing perceptions of different thoughts, feelings, and ideas promotes change. For example, if a teacher promotes positive experiences with communication and collaboration processes in the classroom, through examples and practice, then the students will develop positive perceptions. It is very possible to change perceptions through learning experiences supported by scientific evidence, especially with health professionals who are used to adapting to new knowledge and scientific findings.

Attitudes

An **attitude** is "a relatively enduring organization of beliefs, feelings, and behavioral tendencies towards socially significant objects, groups, events, or symbols" (Hogg & Vaughan, 2005, p. 150). In other words, an attitude is a learned inclination to assess things in a certain way (Cherry, 2023a). People evaluate and form attitudes about ideas, people, objects, or activities (Cherry, 2023a). Attitudes are usually positive or negative, but a person can also have mixed or unclear attitudes (Cherry, 2023a). Positive attitudes are associated with good feelings, such as enjoyment and happiness; negative attitudes are related to anger, dislike, and aggressiveness (Cherry, 2023a).

Whether positive or negative, attitudes can be classified as implicit or explicit (Cherry, 2023a). Explicit attitudes are conscious, and implicit attitudes are unconscious (Cherry, 2023a). Attitudes have different components: affective, cognitive, and behavioral (Cherry, 2023a; McLeod, 2023). What someone feels toward a person, object, or issue is the affective component. Beliefs and ideas are part of the cognitive component. How attitudes influence behavior is the behavioral component (Cherry, 2023a; McLeod, 2023).

Here is an example about teamwork in the workplace. The affective component (feelings toward teamwork): "I do not like teamwork; I feel anxious when I have to do it." The cognitive component (beliefs about teamwork): "Teamwork makes me slower and does not help me accomplish my tasks." The behavioral component (behavior toward teamwork): "I will avoid teamwork by not attending the case discussion meetings."

Forming Attitudes

Many circumstances impact attitude formation, such as direct experience, observation, social factors, norms, and roles (Cherry, 2023a). For example, if students learn from their teachers how to communicate and collaborate through positive experiences in the classroom, they will construct good attitudes by direct experience and observation. Another method of creating attitudes is through social factors and norms; for example, teachers may explain that it is expected for health professionals to work as members of interprofessional teams that need to communicate and collaborate, so it is an important part of their role to work effectively with other team members. The students will understand that communication, collaboration, and teamwork are part of their future jobs through social norms and roles.

Combining positive experiences, examples, social factors, norms, roles, and scientific evidence is the best way to produce positive attitudes about communication and teamwork. If norms and roles are known and understood, but active experiences and observations are negative, the contradiction can produce a mixed or negative attitude. For example, if a person's experiences with communication, collaboration, and teamwork are negative, such as when some team members are irresponsible or difficult to work with, they may avoid teamwork even when norms and roles dictate that communication, collaboration, and teamwork are the optimal ways to approach healthcare work.

The Connection Between Collaboration, Communication, and Teamwork

Collaboration happens when people help others accomplish a common goal or project, which can be private or organizational (Ansa et al., 2020; Castañer & Oliveira, 2020). Collaboration is essential for effective teamwork (Ansa et al., 2020; Franklin et al., 2015; Wang et al., 2022; WHO, 2010). Collaboration within the interprofessional team depends on effective communication and quality relationships among healthcare team members

(Tolle et al., 2019). As the complexity of patient care and the presence of multiple comorbidities increase, providing optimal services requires interprofessional collaboration or IPC (Ansa et al., 2020; Franklin et al., 2015; Wang et al., 2022; WHO, 2010).

In daily clinical practice, formal knowledge about collaboration and **interprofessional collaboration** (IPC) blends with informal thoughts about cooperation and teamwork. If attitudes and perceptions are positive, clinicians will construct an environment to support communication within the healthcare team. It is important to note that health professionals may not have been formally taught about interprofessional practice because many educational healthcare programs consider interprofessional communication, interprofessional education (IPE), and IPC as electives (Schneider et al., 2024). Therefore, IPE training and policies are needed in the workplace to build positive perceptions and attitudes toward IPC within the healthcare team.

IPC occurs when different health professionals partner to give quality care to patients, caregivers, and their families (Ansa et al., 2020; Busari et al., 2017; WHO, 2010). Each team member collaborates by offering their unique perspective, expertise, and experience. This combination results in a higher level of care, which is unachievable by only one health professional (Franklin et al., 2015; Wang et al., 2022; WHO, 2010). As everyone offers their best efforts to collaborate, teamwork is enhanced, and goals are accomplished. Every effort to encourage collaboration enables teamwork, optimizes clinical intervention, and improves patient health.

As science evolves, IPC optimizes healthcare. IPC improves management and communication and reduces the duplication of services (Ansa et al., 2020). IPC facilitates continuity of care, creates proper referral patterns, and facilitates effective collaboration during decision-making processes with patients (Epstein, 2014; Wagner, 2000). First, healthcare professionals must comprehend each other's roles, abilities, and expertise. Then, their perception of the necessity for collaboration, communication, and cooperation among the team members will be enhanced. Acknowledging the worth of each team member's contribution to the decision-making processes during daily clinical work is the foundation for collaboration and teamwork, resulting in better quality of care and patient outcomes (Ansa et al., 2020; WHO, 2010).

Creating Positive Attitudes, Perceptions and Experiences

To develop effective collaborative skills, health professionals should have positive experiences with and attitudes toward IPC (Ansa et al., 2020). To create a positive IPC environment and optimize patient outcomes, healthcare professionals and students must undergo IPE (Spaulding et al., 2019; Wang et al., 2022; WHO, 2010). IPE will promote positive attitudes about and perceptions of IPC and explain how it is essential to optimize patient outcomes and quality of care (Schneider et al., 2024). Clinicians can learn about IPE at any stage of their careers or as students through courses, workshops, simulations, online education, and conferences. Universities and health institutions must facilitate IPE to establish a clear understanding of the relevance and necessity of IPC (Ansa et al., 2020; Schneider et al., 2024; Spaulding et al., 2019; Wang et al., 2022; WHO, 2010).

Core Competencies for Interprofessional Practice: The Relevance of Communication

The World Health Organization (2010) provided a framework to explain the relevance of collaboration and teamwork and to assist health professionals with their practice. Later, the Interprofessional Education Collaborative (IPEC) created a document to promote national conversations about interprofessional collaboration and education and explained the core competencies for successful interprofessional practice (Ansa et al., 2022; IPEC, 2016).

Health educators, administrators, and health organizations must create policies and implement practices through IPE to address the challenges of IPC and develop core competencies in professionals and students (Ansa et al., 2022). Creating specific policies and practices will optimize patient outcomes and improve public health through the continued advancement of science.

The core competencies for Interprofessional Collaborative Practice are values/ethics, roles/responsibilities, interprofessional communication, teams, and teamwork (Ansa et al., 2020; IPEC, 2016). Ethics and values refer to work that reflects mutual respect and adherence to clinical professional standards within professions. Clinicians are expected to carry out their own roles and responsibilities morally and respectfully for the benefit of the population (IPEC, 2016). Communication, teams, and teamwork competencies are used to operationalize values so members can connect effectively with one another, patients, families, and communities (IPEC, 2016). Practicing the four competencies will optimize clinical practice and produce high-quality care that benefits patients and the public (IPEC, 2016).

The Relevance of Communication

Communication within the interprofessional team is essential for effective collaboration during interprofessional practice, especially in critical and complex situations (Wang et al., 2022) when IPC is most beneficial. Studies show that communication within the healthcare team is important and that learning about communication increases students' confidence to engage in IPC (Wang et al., 2022). Health professionals ranked interprofessional communication as the highest core competency for interprofessional practice (Ansa et al., 2020). Other studies found that members of interprofessional teams expressed having the highest anxiety levels while communicating with their teams (Enlow et al., 2010; Thomas et al., 2017; Wang et al., 2015). Recent nursing graduates reported a lack of understanding and knowledge about communication within interprofessional teams and a fear of not being able to communicate clearly, accurately, and fluently during critical situations (Thomas et al., 2009; Velji et al., 2008;). Interprofessional communication training and education supports IPC and optimizes patient health.

Reflective Analysis: Attitudes and Perceptions Scenario

A real-life healthcare teamwork example will be reviewed to analyze attitudes and perceptions regarding communication and collaboration. This situation had two stages: first, between the clinical coordinator and the physical therapist (PT), and second, when the rehabilitation manager called a larger interprofessional team meeting because she did not agree with the PT's decision to provide PT visits without checking in with the IPC team. The analysis process will begin using Kolb's Experiential Learning Perspective (Kolb, 1984; McLeod, 2024a). Then, Maslow's Hierarchy of Needs (McLeod, 2024b) will be applied to explain the behaviors.

Interprofessional Work Case

⁂ Kolb's Learning Perspective Stages ⁂

1) **Concrete Experience**
   Joanne, the clinical coordinator, received a medical order for physical therapy services. She discussed the new case and assigned it to Esther, a PT. Esther, who works per diem, agreed to perform

the initial evaluation. The main goals of the assessment were to determine if skilled services were needed, create a plan of care (POC), and complete the admission (start of care) process. The procedure included evaluating the patient and determining if the case complied with policies and regulations to make the admission. Esther received the case and scheduled her visit with the patient's son the next day.

As soon as Esther arrived at the patient's home and started the evaluation process, she discovered that the patient was going to start her first round of chemotherapy the next week to treat an active cancer diagnosis. This information had not been included in the medical order and patient history provided by the physician's team to Joanne and sent to Esther. The agency's policy was to have a compulsory interprofessional team discussion during admission and discharge to discuss all significant changes and relevant findings in the patient's status. This policy reflected scientific evidence supporting the need for interprofessional work to optimize clinical outcomes and populations' health (Ansa et al., 2020; Franklin et al., 2015; Wang et al., 2022; WHO, 2010). It is important to note that chemotherapy usually results in adverse effects that may interfere with a patient's activities and produce nausea, pain, fragility, and tiredness, which usually require rest.

When Esther discovered the new information about the patient, she decided not to call the rehabilitation manager, Aida, to discuss the case interprofessionally. Instead, she continued the evaluation process and admitted the patient. Esther sent her written report through email to Aida so she could assign a PT assistant to provide the PT treatment intervention she had prescribed. When Aida read Esther's report, she disagreed with Esther's decision to admit the patient.

Aida called the patient's son to inquire about the patient's status and the chemotherapy. The son expressed concern about his mother receiving PT while having chemotherapy. Aida told the patient's son she would bring the case to an interprofessional team discussion to ensure the patient's well-being was addressed. Aida called the clinical manager, a nurse, the quality services coordinator, a PT, and the head of the billing department to discuss the case in detail. Aida asked the interprofessional team to discuss the PT report and her own concern about the patient's endurance and well-being while receiving PT intervention and undergoing chemotherapy. Together, the team concluded that it was better to put the admission on hold until the patient received the chemotherapy and to restart the admission process after the rounds of chemotherapy ended.

Aida called the patient's son to explain the interprofessional team's decision to hold PT services until the chemotherapy ended. He understood and was happy with the decision. Aida notified Esther about the results of the interprofessional team discussion. During the discussion with Aida, Esther expressed that she had decided not to bring the case for discussion with the interprofessional team because she felt she could accomplish her daily tasks faster by managing the case herself. The administrator was pushing clinicians to see more patients and work faster.

Aida reminded Esther about the agency's policy of compulsory case discussions. She told Esther that in the future, she should remember that her job required her to discuss every case with the interprofessional team to promote the best health services. Aida explained how scientific evidence supported that communication, collaboration, and teamwork optimized services and ensured patients' maximal benefit and outcomes. Esther expressed that she understood that case discussions were a policy and a requirement and she would adhere to them in the future.

2) **Reflective Observation**
When Esther, the physical therapist, found out about the missing information in the medical order, she should have called the physical therapy manager, Aida, to discuss her findings about the active cancer diagnosis and the chemotherapy. The policies and regulations of the agency require clinicians to discuss all the cases with the healthcare team to ensure optimal services are provided to their patients. Esther's attitudes toward and perceptions of communication and collaboration were negative. She thought that even though scientific evidence supports IPC and policies at her agency make case discussions a requirement, she could still ignore the regulations to work faster. Esther was task-oriented; maybe she preferred to spend minimal time per case to be cost-effective and to be able to visit more patients per day. She did not value the scientific evidence that supported the need for communication, collaboration, and teamwork because she believed that case discussions were a waste of time.

It is important to note that Esther's initial training as a PT did not include interprofessional education. She also received Aida's new patient care recommendation positively (see Maslow's analysis below). Esther complied with the rest of the requirements.

3) **Abstract Conceptualization**

    a. What happened? Esther, the physical therapist, discovered new evidence about the patient that could impact their well-being and health but decided not to discuss the case with the agency's interprofessional team. She made an incorrect clinical decision. The rehabilitation manager, Aida, discovered the error in clinical judgment when she read the PT report and brought the case to the attention of the interprofessional team, which decided to put the admission on hold until the patient had completed chemotherapy.

    b. What went wrong? Esther did not discuss the case with the team nor comply with the agency's regulations and policies. Her attitudes and perceptions about the benefits of communication, collaboration, and teamwork were negative. Her decision was overridden by the interprofessional team, which decided to put the admission on hold.

    c. What should they do next time to improve communication and collaboration? Esther should attend a communication workshop to help her understand the value of communication and collaboration. In addition, she should follow regulations and procedures for interprofessional case discussions. The rehabilitation manager should continue supervising all clinical work to promote optimal services and outcomes. Esther decided to work faster to meet the administrator's expectations. The administrator wanted clinicians to work with as many patients as possible to increase profits. It's a paradox, but safety and optimal services are the main goals of clinical work. In the end, case discussions will save time by ensuring optimal services are provided and preventing errors.

    d. How can they promote positive attitudes toward and perceptions of communication and collaboration within the team? The agency should summon the clinicians to daily communication huddles; schedule a communication workshop for all the staff; and explain the scientific evidence showing that communication, collaboration, and teamwork promote optimal services and outcomes. Clinicians should discuss all cases frequently to create a habit of communication and feedback. Team members should be invited to casual team-building activities to facilitate positive attitudes about and perceptions of communication and collaboration.

4) **Active Experimentation**

The clinicians should apply their learned concepts about perceptions and attitudes and the value of communication and collaboration during small team meetings. The meetings can be arranged to discuss successful and challenging cases and review the importance of communication and collaboration within the healthcare team. Each clinician should have the opportunity to practice communication and collaboration skills.

The clinical educator or the quality assurance coordinator of the agency may design an evidence-based educational booklet, a video, or a PowerPoint presentation about the relevance of communication and collaboration in preventing errors and promoting optimal services and outcomes. Role-playing workshop activities could be performed among the clinicians to facilitate communication and collaboration.

Moreover, the clinical manager can implement daily huddles and show good leadership characteristics such as empathy, respect, camaraderie, innovation, energy, and enthusiasm to increase motivation, trust, communication, and collaboration among the team members. These activities can improve attitudes toward and perceptions of communication and collaboration. In addition, the manager should establish that their workplace is a safe communication space. She can introduce frequent feedback into the organization's culture. This way, the team will get used to professional input and team reviews, especially when patient outcomes and audits are unsuccessful. Additionally, the clinical manager can ask the organization's upper management to provide workshop opportunities and fraternization activities for all the staff to increase trust and psychological safety and improve attitudes about communication and collaboration. For other strategies, go back to chapter five.

Through practice, team members will gradually perceive communication, collaboration, and feedback as learning processes to improve their outcomes as a group and not take the responses personally, which will increase trust and psychological safety.

⚜ MASLOW'S HIERARCHY OF NEEDS ⚜

This scenario can be analyzed using two different levels in Maslow's Hierarchy: safety needs and self-esteem needs. The second level in Maslow's Hierarchy of Needs, safety needs, describes personal security, resources, health, property, and employment (Maslow, 1943; Maslow, 1954; McLeod, 2024b). Every worker values their job security so they can afford all their needs. The fourth level is self-esteem, which describes the need for respect of and by others, achievement, confidence, and being a unique individual (Maslow, 1943; Maslow, 1954; McLeod, 2024b). Review Figure 3 (pg. 16) for a visual depiction of Maslow's Hierarchy of Needs (McLeod, 2024b).

Every person wants to excel at their job and demonstrate the quality of their performance so they can maintain their employment and fulfill their safety needs in Maslow's Hierarchy. Esther, the physical therapist, wanted to visit as many patients as possible to maximize her productivity and profits for the agency. When Esther was called for a discussion by Aida, the rehabilitation manager, to remind her about compulsory case discussions, she expressed that she would follow policies and regulations in the future as required to prevent the termination of her job (Maslow, 1943; Maslow, 1954; McLeod, 2024b).

At the same time, the scenario can be analyzed using the self-esteem needs level (Maslow, 1943; Maslow, 1954; McLeod, 2024b). Esther demonstrated her autonomy and uniqueness by executing her decisions without discussing the case as required. She wanted to establish her confidence, individuality, and initiative to earn the respect of coworkers at the agency. Even though the behavior was not permitted by the agency, Esther's motivation was aligned with her self-esteem needs.

Educational Activities

This section is an essential part of the learning journey throughout the book. These activities will encourage you to reflect and consider more profound personal experiences. Perform each activity carefully to optimize your communication skills. You can do the learning activities individually, in pairs, or with your professional team. To facilitate the activities, a template was designed to be printed by the readers. It can be used as a visual-motor aid when working on communication examples. The template is included in Appendix A.

Role-Playing: Design Scenarios

a. Reflect on the meaning of perceptions and attitudes. Think of examples based on your experiences with your team members. Do you have coworkers who don't like to communicate and collaborate with the team? Do you have colleagues who interfere with communication and collaboration processes? Create a hypothetical team meeting or discussion to practice behaviors that may occur in these situations. Then, analyze the hypothetical meeting and consider what could be done differently to promote positive perceptions of and attitudes toward communication and collaboration. Go back to Kolb's Experiential Learning Perspective to identify and review the behaviors. Recall the experience, reflect on it, analyze it, and practice using what you've learned.

b. Recall past experiences of ineffective communication that evidenced negative attitudes toward and perceptions of communication and collaboration in one or more of the members of your interprofessional team or study group. Recall each member's contributions during the experiences and make notes. Reflect and discuss with a colleague the negative attitudes and perceptions and their effects on group communication. What elements made the communication ineffective? Think about ways to facilitate communication, collaboration, psychological safety, and trust within your team. Go back to Kolb's Experiential Learning Perspective. Recall the experience, reflect on it, analyze it, and plan for future situations.

c. Recall, reflect on, explain, and analyze examples of the benefits of effective communication and how you can make people feel comfortable during meetings in general. Go to the administrative sector of your job to explain how Medical Improv workshops, fraternization activities, and daily briefs or huddles would improve communication and trust within the team. Share the evidence-based results of good communication practices.

Reflection Points

- ➤ Think about communication and collaboration. Explain what they mean to you and give examples of how they improve teamwork and patient services.
- ➤ Describe positive and negative perceptions of and attitudes toward communication and collaboration. Recall situations where you have worked with people with positive or negative attitudes and consider how they impacted teamwork and outcomes. Give examples.
- ➤ What are positive teamwork, collaboration, and communication behaviors? Recall past experiences and give examples.
- ➤ Is the environment during your meetings at work welcoming to open communication and collaboration?
- ➤ Think about attitudes, perceptions, and behaviors. Do team members' behavior change depending on who is at a meeting?
- ➤ Is there a powerful person who interferes with the communication processes during your team meetings? What are the behaviors they engage in?
- ➤ Analyze the best way to improve communication and collaboration within your team.
- ➤ Are the upper levels of your organization's hierarchy open to communication from clinicians and staff? Do they practice an open-door policy?
- ➤ Think about ways to improve understanding, compatibility, and camaraderie among your team members.

As you read other chapters, you can return to these examples to assess your learning process and see if you can solve the situations differently. In addition, you can recall other experiences from your past using the template in Appendix A. Practice will promote deeper understanding and improve your communication skills.

Further Reading

1) **Ansa, B. E., Zechariah, S., Gates, A. M., Johnson, S. W., Heboyan, V., & De Leo, G.** (2020). *Attitudes and behavior towards interprofessional collaboration among healthcare professionals in a large academic medical center.* Healthcare, 8(3), 323. https://doi.org/10.3390/healthcare8030323.
2) **Castañer, X., & Oliveira, N.** (2020). *Collaboration, coordination, and*

cooperation among organizations: Establishing the distinctive meanings of these terms through a systematic literature review. Journal of Management, 46(6), 965–1001. https://doi.org/10.1177/0149206320901565.

3) **Cherry, K.** (2023a, March 11). *The components of attitude definition, formation, changes. Verywell Mind.* https://www.verywellmind.com/attitudes-how-they-form-change-shape-behavior-2795897.

4) **Cherry, K.** (2023b, February 1). *What is perception? Recognizing environmental stimuli through the five senses. Verywell Mind.* https://www.verywellmind.com/perception-and-the-perceptual-process-2795839.

5) **Franklin, C. M., Bernhardt, J. M., Lopez, R. P., Long-Middleton, E. R., & Davis, S.** (2015). *Interprofessional teamwork and collaboration between community health workers and healthcare teams.* Health Services Research and Managerial Epidemiology, 2, 233339281557331. https://doi.org/10.1177/2333392815573312.

6) **Interprofessional Educational Collaborative.** (2016). *Core competencies for interprofessional collaboration: 2016 Update.* https://www.ipecollaborative.org/assets/2016-Update.pdf.

7) **McLeod, S.** (2023, June 13). Components of attitude: ABC Model. Simply Psychology. https://www.simplypsychology.org/attitudes.html.

8) **McLeod, S.** (2024a, February 2). *Kolb's learning styles and experiential learning cycle.* Simply Psychology. https://www.simplypsychology.org/learning-kolb.html.

9) **Schneider, C., Anders, P., & Rotthoff, T.** (2024). *"It is great what we have learned from each other!"–Bedside teaching in interprofessional small groups using the example of Parkinson's disease.* GMS Journal for Medical Education, 41(1). ISSN 2366-5017.

10) **Wang, W., Shen, J., Greene, W. B., Ren, D., & Sherwood, P.** (2022). *The effect of ISBARR on knowledge of and attitudes about interprofessional communication skills among Chinese undergraduate nursing students.* Nurse Education Today, 109, 105207. https://doi.org/10.1016/j.nedt.2021.105207.

11) **World Health Organization.** (2010). *Framework for action on interprofessional education and collaborative practice.* https://www.who.int/publications/i/item/framework-for-action-on-interprofessional-education-collaborative-practice.

CHAPTER EIGHT

Destroying Communication Barriers
and Facilitating Communication

Destroying Communication Barriers and Facilitating Communication

The importance of effective communication within a healthcare team has been thoroughly established in past chapters. Effective communication is fundamental for quality healthcare services (Sharkiya, 2023; Stray et al., 2024). Understanding that interprofessional communication is essential for collaboration within a team is fundamental to optimizing patient outcomes and team interactions (Ansa et al., 2020; Franklin et al., 2015; Wang et al., 2022; WHO, 2010) Interprofessional collaboration is imperative for controlling quality patient care and tackling the increasing expectations of the healthcare system (Schneider et al., 2024). The primary purpose of this chapter is to review strategies to break down communication barriers. Once barriers have been addressed, actions can be taken to facilitate and reinforce effective communication. The ultimate goal of this chapter is to introduce a comprehensive plan for how a healthcare workplace can execute a holistic approach to improve communication within its interprofessional team.

Misunderstandings and errors caused by ineffective communication are avoidable. Communication is a vital process for facilitating teamwork and improving outcomes (Tolle et al., 2019). Prioritizing communication by adopting a strategic plan to educate team members on communication styles and processes is necessary to build effective interprofessional communication skills. Lessons about interprofessional communication are commonly incorporated into a clinician's education using case studies, modules, simulations, and workshops (Foronda et al., 2016; Keller et al., 2013; Velásquez et al., 2022). Interprofessional communication is a strategy that needs to be valued and practiced since it is the main road toward an effective communication process in the workplace. It is a lifelong learning experience that students and clinicians can continue to improve throughout the years. All healthcare workers and organization leaders should strive toward effective interprofessional communication and teamwork in order to optimize health services and improve patient care because these are the most important daily objectives in the workplace.

When health professionals are hired for a new job, they automatically become part of a community of communicators. To integrate successfully into the community at their workplace, they must understand and value the organization's mission, vision, policies, and regulations. However, it is also key for health professionals to learn and respect the varied communication styles among their team members. Each person brings their particular abilities and experiences to the team. Together, they can form a fluent and cohesive team, a modestly functional group, or a dysfunctional knot that interferes with daily tasks, outcomes, and compliance.

Optimal interprofessional communication and collaboration within the healthcare team will produce the best patient health and outcomes (Ansa et al., 2020; Franklin et al., 2015; Wang et al., 2022; WHO, 2010). Interprofessional teams will provide clinical services to their patients to the best of their abilities. A team's performance can be analyzed and measured by how they communicate and collaborate to reach their goals. It can be viewed and explained as a continuum that ranges from totally ineffective to completely fluid communication.

Members of ineffective communication teams have to fight endless noises, barriers, negative attitudes, and perceptions. Team members feel psychologically unsafe to speak up. These teams are investing extra energy into their daily communication struggle to accomplish their goals, causing them to feel tired of the challenge. Moderately effective teams may accomplish their goals by overcoming many psychological and organizational noises and working around behavioral barriers. In highly effective, fluid teams, team members value each other and experience psychological safety. They can freely and confidently employ their speak up and voice behaviors. Team actions will result in optimal outcomes. Prioritizing communication and collaboration will produce the best and most fluid daily teamwork (Ansa et al., 2020; Franklin et al., 2015; Wang et al., 2022; WHO, 2010).

Constructing Effective Communication: Defeating Noises and Barriers from the Author's Perspective

Frequent communication breakdowns, documentation mistakes, and intervention errors among my interprofessional team and work staff motivated me to start a quest to learn about communication. After a full year and a half of studying the literature, conducting interviews, and having discussions with coworkers about their communication failures and experiences, it is necessary to re-examine what we have discovered throughout this learning journey together. We will focus the review on the most relevant barriers that interfere with communication within a healthcare team, then analyze and connect ideas about evidence-based methods to create effective communication strategies for people in the workplace. As adult learners, we can review, understand, analyze, and describe the experiences gained reading, reflecting, and role-playing to apply what we have learned into daily practice (Kolb, 1984; McLeod, 2024a).

In chapter two, we found that one of the first steps to effective communication is recognizing and understanding people's different communication styles and needs. Realizing that each member of the team has their own duties to accomplish motivates team members to help each other complete their multiple tasks and meet their needs. When they recognize the benefits of interprofessional collaboration, reluctant team members will become more open to communication and to helping others in return. Collaborative teamwork will be more effective than individual efforts to reach goals and improve patient outcomes (Ansa et al., 2020; Franklin et al., 2015; Wang et al., 2022; WHO, 2010).

Communication Noise

Communication noise influences how people interpret messages when they talk to others (MacDonald, 2006). The words are objective, but the person's interpretation and analysis of the message can impact its meaning (Velentzas & Broni, 2014). Understanding the variety of communication noises that can interfere with a message's interpretation is another way to improve communication effectiveness. Reviewing the different types of noise and solutions to them will solidify your learning and help you create new courses of action when noise arises.

Physical and Environmental Noises

Physical and environmental noises are also called external noises because they come from other people or equipment in the area, such as people talking near those trying to communicate or background sounds from cars, construction, airplanes, etc. These noises can distract those receiving the messages (Velentzas & Broni, 2014). Noise near meetings should be identified and controlled by moving the meeting somewhere else or asking for cooperation from those making the noise. Planning meetings ahead of time and providing the best possible environment are necessary when a team and an organization value communication.

Psychological Noise

Psychological noise stems from the assumptions and beliefs of an individual. Both the sender and the receiver of the message can be affected by psychological noise. People have biases about race, stereotypes, and reputation (Piaget, 1953; Velentzas, & Broni, 2014). When someone has predetermined ideas about the other person involved in communication and what they will say or why, it interferes with their ability to understand the message. These preexisting ideas are difficult to eliminate, so team members should be aware and consider how their own biases and the biases of others may affect communication (Velentzas & Broni, 2014). The solution to this noise is to be aware of it and to try to intentionally neutralize your personal biases. Bias interferes with communication. Being open to learning about different cultures, ethnicities, and groups is the beginning. The next step is trying to communicate objectively with people who are different from those with whom you usually spend time. Traveling can give you excellent experiences for understanding people's different perspectives.

Semantic Noise

When language is unclear, has grammatical errors, or is too technical, **semantic noise** happens (Velentzas & Broni, 2014). The person talking causes the noise by using wording that is not clear or understandable to the message receiver (Velentzas & Broni, 2014). An example is employing medical jargon that does not match the expertise of the message receiver. It is important to try to use a common language so everyone can understand. The solution is to be aware of the wording you use and be considerate of others. In addition, the message sender should ask the receiver about their interpretation to make sure the message was understood.

Syntactical Noise

Incorrect language use such as syntax errors, incorrect word order in a sentence, verb tense inconsistency, grammar mistakes, and word choice mistakes cause **syntactical noise** (Velentzas & Broni, 2014). Incorrect use of language interrupts communication and distracts the receiver of the message (Velentzas & Broni, 2014), who will try to correct the message mentally or will feel annoyed. To avoid this syntactical noise, the message sender should plan the communication to prevent errors. Thinking about the sentences that we are going to use before talking helps us make fewer language errors. In addition, discussing the message with a different person ahead of time to evaluate clarity can be a solution. Another way to avoid this noise is for the receiver of the incorrect language to ask the message sender to say the message using different words (i.e., to paraphrase).

Organizational Noise

Organizational noise occurs when an organization's vision, mission, policies, hierarchies, objectives, responsibilities, and specific roles of the employees are not clear, which causes poorly structured communication (Velentzas & Broni, 2014). Because the organization's messages are unclear, employees lack information about what is expected from them and with whom they should communicate, which frustrates the workers. During interviews with many of my (the author's) colleagues, they expressed their experiences with bosses who hired people using false promises or half-truths, which felt like a sales pitch. Such behaviors are counterproductive and interfere with communication. Lack of honesty is discovered sooner or later, and its effect on attitudes toward and perceptions of the organization is catastrophic because trust is broken for the new employee. The solution to this kind of noise is honesty. Organization leaders should know that the truth will always prevail because employees will discover deceit and will probably quit to find a happier and more transparent workplace.

Communication Barriers

Communication effectiveness can be affected by various elements (Guttman et al., 2021). Communication can be complicated by different people with their diverse communication styles, points of view, and backgrounds, as well as the complex nature of the healthcare setting (Fausett et al., 2024). Barriers such as cultural and linguistic differences and information overload affect communication (Gluyas, 2015). It is important to remember that power disparities and hierarchical structures in healthcare organizations interfere with communication, collaboration, decision-making, and overall team achievement (Stevens et al., 2021). For more details about power balance, please go back to chapter six. The causes of communication breakdowns can be classified into causal barriers: cognitive, linguistic, environmental, technological, and behavioral (Guttman et al., 2021). We will review the barriers in this section, but you can go back to chapter three for more details.

Cognitive Barriers

Cognitive barriers are produced when a message lacks information or context or has unnecessary and distracting information (Guttman et al., 2021). This could be caused by a variety of things: trying to convey too much information at once, feeling anxious while communicating, or running out of time for a conversation. In these cases, information is not carried from sender to receiver properly, which interferes with understanding and attention levels. Communication barriers related to cognition create distractions and interruptions for both the sender and receiver of the message that hinder the perception and processing of the message (Guttman et al., 2021).

Cognitive barriers can be caused by environmental barriers such as background noise. Mixed cognitive and environmental barriers are common in real-life situations. For example, a message can lack information and the people communicating can be anxious because of workload or burnout (cognitive barriers), and at the same time, the communicators can be talking in a noisy place (environmental barrier). For more details about environmental barriers, see the section on linguistic barriers below.

To prevent cognitive barriers, it is important to be organized during communication and to plan what you're going to say. Think about what will be said beforehand, select the correct words, and consider other barriers that may cause communication breakdown. Move toward a quiet place if available. Reinforcing awareness about the importance of complete and clear messages during communication can help. In stressful situations, taking time to center yourself, breathe, and relax is a practical strategy to reduce cognitive barriers.

Linguistic Barriers

Communication breakdowns caused by issues with speech components and their structure are known as **linguistic barriers** (Guttman et al., 2021). Elements of linguistic barriers include tone, speech style, rhythm, word order and choice, voice fluctuations, speech, word meaning, jargon, idioms, metaphors, context, grammar, and similar-sounding words (Guttman et al., 2021).

Employing medical jargon and technical terms when speaking with others who do not share your expertise is a linguistic issue; another is using figures of speech and idioms that the message receiver cannot understand (Guttman et al., 2021). Talking too fast, pauses, and unclear word use can be avoided by planning the language that you will utilize. Paying attention to the importance of tone, rhythm, word meaning, and word choice will help you avoid this communication barrier.

Environmental Barriers

Environmental barriers are caused by coworkers' conversations, equipment, machinery, tools, alarms, and sounds in the place where communication is happening (Hasfeldt et al., 2010). Other investigators categorize environmental barriers as noises, so they are mentioned above as physical and environmental noises. Sounds and noticeable noises interfere with the reception and transmission of a message. As mentioned before, cognitive barriers are frequently connected to environmental barriers because audible noises may interfere with the understanding and interpretation of messages. When noises interfere with interpretation, an environmental barrier triggers the cognitive barrier. As with physical and environmental noises, solutions include planning meetings ahead of time and providing the best possible environment. When environmental barriers happen by surprise, moving the meeting somewhere else is the best option.

Technological Barriers

Technological barriers are caused by technology. For example, the use of electronic medical records (EMR) distracts health professionals when they interact with patients, affects team communication negatively, slows patient care, and promotes illness (Guttman et al., 2021). Technological barriers happen when students, faculty, or clinicians have trouble uploading or downloading data to the EMR. Use of the EMR interferes with face-to-face communication between staff and patients and delays the intervention with the patient (Guttman et al., 2021) In addition, the EMR format separates provider notes per discipline which may negatively impact the detection of critical illnesses and affects patients' health (Hoonakker et al., 2013). This EMR technological interference can happen when clinicians don't check or cannot find relevant information in the separated sections of the EMR.

Although using texting and group chats is common within health professional teams to communicate, it may cause another technological barrier. Messaging about work issues may interrupt the face-to-face interaction with the patient, family members, caregivers, and health team. As these chats and texts disturb the clinician's mindset during the intervention, these interruptions may cause and combine with other communication barriers such as cognitive, behavioral, and environmental.

Behavioral Barriers

One of the most relevant communication barriers is being silent within the healthcare team. Communication starts when team members declare their ideas. A **behavioral communication barrier** happens when people remain silent rather than speaking up to communicate or voicing their thoughts out loud

(Guttman et al., 2021). Persons who don't express themselves may have a fear of committing mistakes or being judged as incompetent or inept (Guttman et al., 2021). Others keep quiet to avoid past undesirable experiences (Milliken & Morrison, 2003). To promote speak up and voice behavior psychological safety (Ge, 2020) and trust should be increased within the team (Hamilton et al., 2024; Steward, 2023).

Psychological safety occurs when people feel that they can talk without fear of consequences to their career, prestige, or self-image (Edmondson, 1999; Kahn, 1990a). In this environment, there is a feeling of comfort and safety within a group, and they are confident that their actions will bring no hurt (Fausett et al., 2024). The desire to communicate outweighs the fear of negative reactions (Jamal et al., 2023). Trust is a feeling that people around an individual will behave in their favor (CIPD, 2012; Edmondson et al., 2004). Correspondingly, trust is a precursor of psychological safety, which means that for an environment to be psychologically safe, people must feel trust within it (Hamilton et al., 2024). Healthcare leaders play an essential role in the team to facilitate psychological safety (Fausett et al., 2024). Leaders should provide support, act friendly, and encourage communication to increase psychological safety (Remtulla et al., 2021). In addition, for team leaders to promote an open culture, they must value the ideas and opinions of all team members (Fausett et al., 2024). For more details about psychological safety and trust, please go back to chapter five.

Communication Facilitators

As we have discussed before, prioritizing communication and being aware of its importance is an essential step toward communication facilitation. Following practical behaviors will facilitate your approach to communication enhancement. Actions toward communication facilitation within the healthcare team should include 1) The use of concise and clear messaging, 2) active empathic listening, and 3) adequate communication tools (Fausett et al., 2024).

Concise and Clear Messaging

The first step is to ensure your message is concise and clear in order to share correct and understandable communication with the team (Fausett et al., 2024). Taking time to remove the communication barriers discussed before will secure transparent and accurate messaging among team members (Guttman et al., 2021). The organization and the team should be aware of and value communication. Moreover, they should give their full attention to creating clear messages and providing feedback about their understanding during their meetings.

Active and Empathic Listening

Active listening is when you pay total attention to what is being said and are completely engaged in the communication process. The purpose of active listening is to ensure you understand the full message. Adding empathy to the listening process takes it to the next level. **Empathy** occurs when people actively put themselves in the other person's position to try to feel what the other feels. Active listening and empathy should be practiced among the team members, colleagues, patients, and stakeholders to facilitate communication (Fausett et al., 2024). Taking all these aspects into account will help you build trust and deepen relationships to develop comprehension of individual concerns and needs among the people (Fausett et al., 2024).

Suitable Communication Tools

Some organizations design their communication tools according to their specific needs and regulations. Examples are group discussion templates and patient data collection forms that ensure minimal analysis and include the required information. Using the correct communication tools, such as messaging platforms, telemedicine technologies, and the electronic medical record (EMR), will support effective communication (Fausett et al., 2024). Additionally, tools should enable secure and efficient communication while also protecting patient privacy (Fausett et al., 2024).

Adaptative Leadership

As mentioned before, the way that leaders behave in their team affects psychological safety and communication effectiveness (Fausett et al., 2024; Remtulla et al. (2021). In today's fast-changing conditions, leadership must adapt to the evolving healthcare team's needs (Fausett et al., 2024). In a study performed by Fausett et al. (2024), the investigators combined the adaptative leadership behaviors of Heifetz et al. (2009) and the factors that influenced team effectiveness identified by Tannenbaum and Salas (2020) with their own academic leadership experiences. This allowed them to create a practical framework that emphasizes what leaders should address in order to work effectively with their healthcare team.

Fausett et al. (2024) recommended that to accomplish cohesive and successful teamwork, healthcare team leaders must apply and promote five key insights. First of all, leaders must support the wellness of healthcare providers using intentional and transparent communication to decrease feelings of isolation, guide the team through change, and promote adaptation to their new goals. Adaptative leaders must promote psychological safety, team cohesion, and communication; leverage transitive memory systems; and practice leadership sharing among team members (Fausett et al., 2024). Evidence suggests that these qualities are strong predictors of team performance in healthcare environments (Boak et al., 2015; Johnson, 2019; O'Donovan & McAuliffe, 2020b; Sanko, 2015; VanVactor, 2012). Strategies to facilitate psychological safety and communication were already discussed. Other insights to facilitating cohesive teamwork to optimize success will be discussed in the following sections.

Promoting Team Cohesion

Team cohesion, defined as "the forces acting on the members to remain in the team" (Festinger, 1950, p. 11), is essential for successful teamwork (Carron & Brawley, 2000; Lott & Lott, 1965) and high-quality healthcare services (Fausett et al., 2024). Team cohesion implies collaboration, unity, a common purpose, effective communication, respect, and mutual trust among health professionals (DeeterSchmelz & Norman Kennedy, 2003). In common words, cohesion is the glue that keeps the team together. A group that has good team cohesion will communicate and collaborate effectively (Fausett et al., 2024).

To facilitate team cohesion, it is essential to have peer support, internal control, clear roles, and common team objectives (Fausett et al., 2024). Moreover, transparency during communication, common team goals, and shared expectations assist the team in moving toward a common purpose (Mickan & Rodger, 2005). Agreeableness, which is a personality trait, is an influential factor in fostering cohesion (Acton, 2019). Team cohesion is the togetherness of the group. This togetherness must be cultivated by the team leader and by each of the team's members to facilitate teamwork and collaboration to achieve the team's maximal potential.

Leveraging Transactive Memory Systems

Transactive memory systems (TMS) refer to the collective memory of the organization and define what each of the organization's members knows

(Argote et al., 2018; van Lamoen et al., 2023). A team's knowledge, trust, gender diversity, absence of conflict within the team, and group potency contribute to the formation of TMS (He & Hu, 2021; Prichard & Ashleigh, 2007). TMS is a way of sharing collective knowledge among team members (Lewis, 2003) so they can learn from each other's failures (Fan et al., 2016). Team members can access each other's knowledge to collaborate and align their clinical intervention to accomplish patient goals together (Fausett et al., 2024). Frequent communication and continued team interactions predict TMS (He & Hu, 2021).

TMS team longevity is fostered by minimal turnover or low new member additions, which increase their transactive memory in the team (Lewis, 2003; Lewis et al., 2005). On the other hand, high turnover, organizational changes, lack of psychological safety, and hierarchical structures hinder the transactive memory of the team (Lewis, 2003; Lewis et al., 2005). To facilitate transactive memory, team leaders must encourage knowledge sharing, communication, and collaboration and value each team member's knowledge and experience.

Shared Leadership

Shared leadership happens when the team executes leadership functions together (Fausett et al., 2024). Sharing leadership is an easy concept to understand. It is rather difficult to accomplish especially in classic hierarchical organizations. It is a group construct in which leadership tasks are distributed among team members instead of only a single leader. Leadership actions are performed by many individuals instead of just the formal leaders on the top of the hierarchy (Bligh et al., 2006).

To promote shared leadership, senior management and physician support are critical (Boak et al., 2015). Authoritarian approaches should be avoided (Fausett et al., 2024). A clear and shared group mission is essential to align all team members so they can collaborate and accomplish a common goal. Every team member must recognize and value the contributions of each individual in the team (Fausett et al., 2024). A team leader must be capable of sharing leadership behaviors with team members and facilitating communication, teamwork, and collaboration.

Practical Approaches to Facilitate Communication at an Organization

Prioritizing communication is a decision that every healthcare organization should make because effective communication is the cornerstone of quality healthcare (Sharkiya, 2023). The first step toward optimizing communication at the organizational level is preventing organizational noise. As explained before, organizational noise happens when an organization's mission, vision, policies, and objectives are not clear to the employees and communication with the staff is unclear (Velentzas & Broni, 2014). The employees lack information about their roles and responsibilities, which many feel frustrating.

Healthcare organizations should use clear communication to continually inform their employees about their policies, challenges, accomplishments, procedures, and expectations. This course of action should start as early as the hiring process. The interview process is relevant as it is the first impression that a future employee will have of the company. The organization must promote honesty, transparent communication, and psychological safety (Fausett et al., 2024). All employees should be informed about potential changes and the company's short- and long-term goals. Effective leadership, honesty, and respect that show employees' needs and ideas are valued by the organization will improve personnel performance, retention, and staff morale (Fausett et al., 2024; Tsarouha et al., 2021)

To optimize communication, team leaders should facilitate understanding about communication, the communication cycle, the communication styles, the skills needed to communicate effectively, effective and ineffective communication, communication noises, and communication barriers. Frequent reflection on and analysis of communication successes and failures will improve awareness and move an organization forward toward communication improvement. To continue learning about teamwork, communication, and collaboration within your team, difficult cases with successes and failures should be discussed among the team members. Frequent workshops about communication, short daily huddles, and meetings will improve communication, teamwork, and performance. Enabling fraternization activities will improve communication and decrease communication barriers.

Prioritizing and Facilitating Communication at the Organization Level

I (the author of this book) have created a list of organizational activities for prioritizing communication within an interprofessional team. It is important to note that the primary and ongoing requirement for optimizing communication is providing a psychologically safe environment in the workplace. For details about psychological safety, please go back to chapter five. The list provided is a practical tool to help design a new approach for optimizing interprofessional communication. As each company has its own organizational culture, the activities can be modified to suit their unique needs.

➤ **Recruiting Personnel**
- Prepare for an interview with questions to ask the candidate that reflect the organization's mission, vision, expectations, ethics, and emphasis on interprofessional communication
- Emphasize the assessment of communication styles and skills during the interview.
    - Ask questions to assess positive or negative attitudes toward and perceptions of communication and teamwork.
    - Example questions:
        ➤ What is your favorite method of communication?
        ➤ What do you think about interprofessional communication?
    - Introduce clinical scenarios for the candidate to solve. Analyze the candidate's answers to assess their attitudes toward and perceptions of communication.

➤ **Onboarding Process**
- Offer comprehensive education about all the requirements of the job to new hires. This way, the clinician can understand the organization's mission, vision, policies, regulations, and clinical record documentation as well as the value of communication, collaboration, and teamwork.
- Provide opportunities for professional development such as:
    - Interprofessional education
    - Communication workshops

➤ **Case Discussions:**
- Design communication-specific tools to be used during case discussions to collect all the necessary information required by professional standards, state and federal law, health insurance, and the organization's accreditation providers.
- Teach, practice, and use the communication tools during case discussions.

➤ **Continuous Education:**
- Schedule short monthly meetings to discuss employees' issues, recommendations, and educational interests. This will promote active communication among administration and staff.

- Schedule in-service workshops about psychological safety, trust, power dynamics, and adaptive leadership to promote effective communication within the healthcare team.
- Staff development opportunities: Provide learning opportunities about communication, collaboration, teamwork, interprofessional education, or other topics to benefit team development.

Reflective Analysis: Practical Communication Cases

A description of a real example will be used to analyze communication processes and how they were facilitated or hindered. The situations occurred among interprofessional team members. The analysis process will begin using Kolb's Experiential Learning Perspective (Kolb, 1984; McLeod, 2024a). Then, Maslow's Hierarchy of Needs (McLeod, 2024b) will be applied to explain the behaviors.

Intake Communication Failure

⪊ KOLB'S LEARNING PERSPECTIVE STAGES ⪉

1) **Concrete Experience**
   Yolanda, a registered nurse who had been working for the last fifteen years in a home health agency, was actively recruited by another home health agency. She was attracted to the new job opportunity because human resources made an excellent offer. During the face-to-face interview, the chief of the department of human resources, Juan, promised a large number of patient visits which would ensure a higher income. In addition, Juan explained that she was going to visit patients near her home, which would decrease her time in the field and car expenditures. She discussed the better job conditions with her husband and accepted the position as a per diem clinician at the new agency. Yolanda was such a good clinician that many of her patients from the other agency refused services there and chose to become clients of the new agency so they could continue receiving healthcare from their favorite nurse.
   As soon as Yolanda arrived, she went through a short educational intake with the agency. Jane, the clinical manager, explained that the educational process was going to be short since she was a seasoned home health clinician. Yolanda could start

working as soon as possible. Jane added that the number of patients was high, so human resources needed her to start with her patients the next day. Jane kindly offered her support during the training and expressed that if Yolanda felt that she needed assistance or more information about the agency's policies, regulations, and evaluation tools, she would be available. They would continue the education as a learning-by-doing process. Yolanda agreed and happily started working with her patients.

A week after Yolanda's intake, a nurse from the agency surprisingly quit. The human resources director gave instructions to assign her patients to Yolanda. The patients were far from Yolanda's home, but the director assured her that the work was going to be temporary. Yolanda accepted the new patients away from her route.

When Yolanda started to discharge her patients due to accomplishing their goals, she observed that no new patients were assigned to her. After talking to other nurses, she learned that two new nurses had been hired. The other nurses expressed that the new hires were personal friends of the clinical coordinator nurse, Joana. Joana was in charge of assigning the cases to the clinicians. She assigned patients to her friends and not to Yolanda. The agreement about the temporary change of route was not honored by the organization. Yolanda continued working far from home with just a few patients because the clinical coordinator was assigning the new patients to her friends.

Weeks after Yolanda's intake, the auditors expressed to Jane, the clinical manager, that there were issues with the documentation of Yolanda's patient notes. She was still in training, so Yolanda received some continuing education from Jane to improve her documentation, and it was effective. It is important to note that Jane quit her clinical manager position some weeks later after providing documentation re-education to Yolanda.

Six months later, Yolanda was still visiting the patients far from her house and her patient roster was very small. Her income was not enough for her family responsibilities, so she decided to quit since she had a good offer in another clinical setting. Before quitting, Yolanda asked for a brief exit meeting with Jane, the former clinical manager, and explained the situation to her. She expressed that everything that had happened was unfair. Yolanda thanked Jane for the kind personal support and honesty, but said her decision was irreversible. The new manager was unaware of the difficulties that Yolanda had experienced during her time at the organization and the favoritism of the clinical coordinator. Yolanda decided not to include the details of her reasons for quitting the agency in her resignation letter.

2) **Reflective Observation**

During the hiring process, Yolanda did not receive complete information about her job position. Human resources did not express that she was going to take other nurses' patients if someone quit. The intake process was too short, so Yolanda did not learn the full policies, regulations, and tools needed to perform her job. The favoritism practiced by the clinical coordinator was unknown by the clinical manager and by human resources, which is evidence of a lack of communication among the personnel. Moreover, there was a lack of speak up behavior from Yolanda. She decided to keep quiet about the issue and monetary distress until she quit. Lack of communication at all levels had negative effects on Yolanda's well-being, which resulted in her resignation.

3) **Abstract Conceptualization**

    a. What happened? Human resources hired Yolanda using incomplete information, which resulted in unreal expectations, frustration, and sadness for her.

    b. What went wrong? Yolanda received incomplete information during the hiring process. The intake process was too short. In addition, Yolanda suffered from the favoritism of the clinical coordinator toward other clinicians. She was disappointed and sad because she'd left a stable position only to experience the consequences of misinformation—organizational noise. She felt betrayed by the company, the human resources department and its director, and the clinical coordinator. She said that her experience was unfair.

    c. What should they do next time to improve communication and collaboration? Human resources should use transparent communication to avoid organizational noise during hiring and promote the well-being of personnel. This would decrease turnover rates in the company. Yolanda, on the other hand, should have asked questions about possible situations, how the cases are assigned, and what would be expected of her. She should use her voice behavior in the future.

     d.   How can they promote positive attitudes toward and perceptions of communication and collaboration among the team members? The agency should use transparent and complete information during the hiring process. Human resources personnel should partake in a workshop about organizational noise, psychological safety, and the importance of clear and concise communication. Furthermore, the organization should assess their staff's well-being by conducting frequent interviews performed by the human resources personnel to understand their employees' challenges and needs. Then, they should analyze the results to try to improve their staff's work conditions.

4) **Active Experimentation**

Clinicians should apply the learned concepts about the importance of transparent clear and concise communication. They should understand how incomplete information and organizational noise may negatively impact team cohesion and have a devastating effect on trust. Yolanda should practice speaking up and learn about the importance of expressing her needs and challenges. She could have had assistance from the clinical manager to solve the situation.

The ex-manager should go and talk to the new clinical manager and expose the favoritism shown by the clinical coordinator to correct the issue. This situation may cause the resignation of other clinicians in the future. This way, the new clinical manager can talk to the clinical coordinator and the administrators to improve communication and increase psychological safety and trust within the team.

The clinical manager can implement daily huddles and show good leadership characteristics such as empathy, respect, camaraderie, innovation, energy, and enthusiasm to increase motivation, trust, communication, and collaboration within the team. In addition, the clinical manager can learn about adaptative leadership through a workshop to improve her leadership skills so she can detect when a clinician is struggling and provide help.

These activities can improve attitudes toward and perceptions of communication and collaboration. In addition, the clinical manager should establish that their workplace is a safe communication space. She could introduce frequent feedback into the organization's culture. This way, the team will get used to professional input and team reviews, especially when patient outcomes and audits are unsuccessful.

Through practice, leaders and team members will gradually perceive communication, collaboration, and feedback as a learning processes to improve their outcomes as a group and not take the responses personally, which will increase trust and psychological safety.

⚜ Maslow's Hierarchy of Needs ⚜

This scenario can be analyzed using the second level of Maslow's Hierarchy: safety needs. This stage describes personal security, resources, health, property, and employment (Maslow, 1943; Maslow, 1954; McLeod, 2024b). Every worker values their job security so they can afford all their needs. Yolanda changed her workplace, as she was looking for a higher salary and a convenient patient route near her house. That way, her expenses in gasoline and car use would decrease. She was pursuing an improvement in salary and time availability for her family when she accepted the new position.

Human resources personnel actions can be analyzed from the same perspective. They needed to hire a nurse as soon as possible to satisfy their safety need of employment for themselves and for the agency, which needed a nurse very soon. They used a "sales pitch" message that every person wants to hear: a convenient route, more patients, and a higher salary. Their message was incomplete in order to "sell" the position to Yolanda. In the end, she discovered that the job offer had not been transparent from the start, which resulted in her resignation. Review Figure 3 (pg. 16) for a visual depiction of Maslow's Hierarchy of Needs (McLeod, 2024b).

Educational Activities

This section is a crucial part of the learning throughout the book. These activities will encourage you to reflect and consider more profound personal experiences. Perform each activity carefully to optimize your communication skills. You can do the learning activities individually, in pairs, or with your professional team. To facilitate the activities, a template was designed to be printed by the readers. It can be used as a visual-motor aid when working on communication examples. The template is included in Appendix A.

Role-Playing: Design Scenarios

    a.   Think about and discuss communication noises and how to eliminate them. Remember physical, environmental, psychological, syntactical, semantic, and organizational noises. Define each one and consider solutions.

b. Think about and discuss communication barriers. Define them and give examples of behavioral, cognitive, technological, environmental, and linguistic barriers. Consider possible solutions.

c. Analyze communication facilitators: psychological safety, team cohesion, open communication, transitive memory systems (TMS), and leadership sharing. Define the concepts and give examples of how to promote communication using each facilitator.

d. Reflect on adaptative leadership and its benefits. Recall past experiences with different leaders in your time as an employee. How did a positive leader motivate you to do your best? How did an authoritarian leader affect your performance? Your speak up behavior? Your trust?

e. Recall experiences of using different communication tools at your workplaces or school. Review how these tools helped or interfered with communication.

f. Analyze how a clear and concise message improves communication. On the other hand, think about people whom you cannot understand and how this affects communication. Share your experiences with your team.

g. Describe how to practice active and empathic listening. Give examples. Review how it fosters communication.

h. Think about the organization or university that you are a part of. Do they facilitate communication? Is the faculty or management open to communication? Do you think that the organization needs to improve? Review the recommendations in this book and consider solutions. Share them with colleagues, fellow students, or faculty. Initiating a discussion can be the first step toward improving communication.

i. Recall past experiences in which an organization caused a lack of psychological safety within your team and someone wanted to talk but felt they could not. The person remained silent. Remember each team member's contributions during the experience and make notes. Reflect and discuss with a colleague and identify what elements made the communication ineffective. Think about ways to improve communication, psychological safety, and trust within your team. Go back to Kolb's Experiential Learning Perspective. Recall the experience, reflect on it, analyze it, and plan for future situations.

j.   Recall, reflect on, explain, and analyze examples about the benefits of adaptative leadership and how the leader can make people feel comfortable during meetings. Go to the administrative sector of your job to explain how workshops, fraternization activities, and daily briefs or huddles would improve communication and trust within the team. Share the evidence-based results of good communication practices.

Reflection Points

➤ Recall communication noises and communication barriers that you have experienced. Discuss these examples with your team.

➤ Consider how you sense trust. Explain trust and give examples.

➤ Describe psychological safety and recall situations in which you have felt safe to speak up. Give examples.

➤ Recall situations when you should have spoken. Why did you remain silent? Think about specific examples and reflect on your experiences.

➤ Do you feel that some people are more receptive to your ideas than others? Do these feelings invite you to use speak up, silence, or voice behaviors? Give examples and analyze each one.

➤ Consider how to increase trust among your healthcare professional team.

➤ Describe and analyze how a leader can contribute to trust and psychological safety within a team.

➤ Recall the teams you have worked with and describe the environment you sensed when working with them. Was the leadership effective? Did it increase trust and psychological safety?

➤ Recall your teamwork at different workplaces in your past and present. What needed to improve? Have you been a part of fluid communication teams, moderately effective teams, or ineffective teams? How does it feel to communicate effectively as a team?

➤ Examine the best way that you can improve communication within your team.

➣ Is the environment during your meetings at work welcoming to open communication?

➣ Are the upper levels of your organization's hierarchy open to communication? Do you feel that they don't care about their staff? Give examples of why you think this way.

➣ Think about ways to improve understanding and compatibility within your team.

➣ Think about ways to improve understanding, communication, and empathy in your organization. How can you contribute?

As you read other chapters, you can return to these educational activities and the example to assess your learning process and see if you can solve the situations differently. In addition, you can recall other experiences from your past using the template in Appendix A. Practice will promote deeper understanding and improve your communication skills.

Further Reading

1) **Ansa, B. E., Zechariah, S., Gates, A. M., Johnson, S. W., Heboyan, V., & De Leo, G.** (2020). *Attitudes and behavior towards interprofessional collaboration among healthcare professionals in a large academic medical center.* Healthcare, 8(3), 323. https://doi.org/10.3390/healthcare8030323.

2) **Edmondson, A.** (1999). *Psychological safety and learning behavior in work teams.* Administrative Science Quarterly, 44(2), 350–383. https://doi.org/10.2307/2666999.

3) **Edmondson, A. C., & Lei, Z.** (2014). P*sychological safety: The history, renaissance, and future of an interpersonal construct.* Annual Review of Organizational Psychology and Organizational Behavior, 1 (1), 23–43. https://doi.org/10.1146/annurev-orgpsych-031413-091305.

4) **Fausett, C. M., Korentsides, J. M., Miller, Z. N., & Keebler, J. R.** (2024). *Adaptive leadership in health care organizations: Five insights to promote effective teamwork.* Psychology of Leaders and Leadership, 27(1), 6–26. https://doi.org/10.1037/mgr0000148.

5) **Ge, Y.** (2020). *Psychological safety, employee voice, and work engagement.* Social Behavior and Personality: An International Journal, 48 (3). https://doi.org/10.2224/sbp.8907.

6) **Guttman, O. T., Lazzara, E. H., Keebler, J. R., Webster, K. L., Gisick, L. M., & Baker, A. L.** (2021). *Dissecting communication barriers in healthcare: A path to enhancing communication resiliency, reliability, and patient safety.* Journal of Patient Safety, 17(8), e1465-e1471. https://doi.org/10.1097/pts.0000000000000541.

7) **Heifetz, R. A., Grashow, A., & Linsky, M.** (2009). *The practice of adaptive leadership: Tools and tactics for changing your organization and the world.* Harvard Business Press.

8) **Stray, K., Wibe, T., Debesay, J., & Bye, A.** (2024). *Older adults' perceptions and experiences of interprofessional communication as part of the delivery of integrated care in the primary healthcare sector: a meta-ethnography of qualitative studies.* BMC Geriatrics, 24(1). https://doi.org/10.1186/s12877-024-04745-4.

9) **Tannenbaum, S., & Salas, E.** (2020). *Teams that work: The seven drivers of team effectiveness.* Oxford University Press.

10) **Tolle, S. L., Vernon, M. M., McCombs, G., & De Leo, G.** (2019). *Interprofessional education in dental hygiene: Attitudes, barriers and practices of program faculty.* American Dental Hygienists' Association, 93(2), 13-22. https://jdh.adha.org/content/93/2/13.full.

11) **Velentzas, J. O. H. N., & Broni, G.** (2014). *Communication cycle: Definition, process, models and examples.* Recent Advances in Financial Planning and Product Development, 17, 117-131. ISBN: 978-1-61804-261-3.

12) **World Health Organization.** (2010). *Framework for action on interprofessional education and collaborative practice.* https://www.who.int/publications/i/item/framework-for-action-on-interprofessional-education-collaborative-practice.

CHAPTER NINE

Improving Communication Through Education and Lifelong Learning

Improving Communication Through Education and Lifelong Learning

Communication is deeper than saying something and being heard by a listener; it is an interaction that involves sharing information among people (Gephart & Cholette, 2012; Guttman et al., 2021). In real-life situations, members of a healthcare interprofessional team need listening and communication skills to accomplish teamwork, problem-solving, leadership, guidance, and effective patient care (INACSL, 2016; Labrague et al., 2018; Reeves et al., 2016). Communication must proceed effectively among the members of the interprofessional team, staff, and patients (Kukko et al., 2020). Throughout this book, we have learned about many communication problems and how they affect patient outcomes. We have discovered communication barriers; speak up, silence, and voice behaviors; adaptive leadership; communication facilitators; learning activities; and practical solutions. In this chapter, we will explore learning, interprofessional education, the interference of ineffective communication with the learning process, and the application of learning to optimize communication.

The Importance of This Book's Learning Process

This textbook's purpose is to provide readers with a practical learning experience about communication within an interprofessional team through analysis, reflection, and practice. Discovering evidence-based solutions and examining different real-life experiences has been a productive journey. Readers can now further enrich their learning process by performing the educational activities at the end of each chapter individually or with their team members. To promote active learning, they should remember and compare and contrast the book's examples with their own experiences as communicators. Then, readers should apply what they've learned to promote behavioral change and optimize communication. They can repeat this process with new experiences and review the outcomes as many times as they want. All the chapters have been written using Kolb's Experiential Learning Perspective (Kolb, 1984; McLeod, 2024a) and Maslow's Hierarchy of Needs (McLeod, 2024b). To review Kolb's and Maslow's theories, go back to chapter one. In this last chapter, other relevant concepts about adult learning will be discussed to enrich this constructive experience.

Health Professionals' Responsibility to Continue Learning

Society keeps moving nonstop in search of breakthroughs in knowledge, science, and technology. Health professions that in the 1980s required a bachelor's degree now require a doctoral degree. Today's huge body of knowledge and the complexity of life make interprofessional teamwork a necessity to provide the best healthcare to all patients (Loria, 2024; O'Leary et al., 2023). Interprofessional teamwork is now a requirement because cooperation, collaboration, and communication are crucial for organizations and their interprofessional teams (Castañer & Oliveira, 2020; Loria, 2024; O'Leary et al., 2023; Wang et al., 2022; WHO, 2010).

However, it is common to encounter clinicians who do not update their practice to align with contemporary practice. During interviews with me (the author), many clinicians expressed that to be able to work, they complied with the license requirements of their professions and kept up with the status quo. They did not learn new and significant professional skills after their graduation.

As health professions evolve, previous theories and skills become obsolete or are exchanged for simpler, more effective ways of thinking and working. Therefore, to remain effective, healthcare practitioners must engage in lifelong learning.

Lifelong Learning

Lifelong learning is a continuous search for wisdom and attainment of abilities that goes past formal education and is critical to staying flexible and competitive at work (Alheit, 2018). It is a major focus of education and its practice and policies (Kilag et al., 2024). Lifelong learning can be accomplished through different experiences and activities such as formal or informal education, self-directed learning activities, and on-the-job training (Sasan & Baritua, 2022). Reading books such as this one and being an active member of professional associations are examples of ways to achieve self-directed learning. Continuous learning and the adapting of skills are essential in present times when the fast-changing environment in the workplace, globalization, and technological shifts demand rapid adjustments and compliance (Sasan & Baritua, 2022).

Promoting Lifelong Learning

Although lifelong learning emphasizes informal education and self-directed learning, it can be promoted through certain practices within formal education. Kilag et al. (2024) revealed that the best teaching methods to develop lifelong learning are experiential learning, reflective practice, collaborative learning, technology integration, and problem-based learning. Kilag et al. (2024) explained:

- ⮞ Experiential learning offers opportunities to apply learning in real-life experiences such as clinical practices, and simulations.
- ⮞ Reflective practice allows you to ponder real experiences to analyze and examine learning to facilitate self-awareness and growth.
- ⮞ Collaborative learning provides opportunities to work in groups, which fosters and encourages a culture of nonstop learning and professional growth.
- ⮞ Technology integration allows you to practice using digital devices and systems to learn the newest tools and resources to allow for professional growth.
- ⮞ Problem-based learning challenges participants to analyze and work collaboratively to find solutions; it can facilitate problem-solving skills, critical thinking, and a positive mindset for lifelong learning.

Learning Technologies

Health professionals must learn and understand the need to use technology as part of their work. The continuous development of learning technologies is aligned with the necessity for lifelong learning. In modern society, technology is omnipresent, including in health professions education, or HPE (Grainger et al., 2024). **Learning technologies** refer to digital technologies used to teach and learn. Their main focus is computer utilization for teaching contemporary practice (Grainger et al., 2024). Examples include learning management systems (Dobre, 2015), live streaming and lecture capture (Biscan et al., 2021), learning analytics solutions (Viberg et al., 2018), web-based or mobile applications for supplementary or self-paced learning (Gladman et al., 2021; Gladman et al., 2023), and artificial intelligence and virtual reality (Kyaw et al., 2019).

Ineffective Communication as a Barrier to Learning

Understanding and practicing the process of effective communication are the keys to promoting effective learning for both students and health professionals. During the learning process, teachers and learners are communicators who send and receive messages about the topics being taught (Muslimin et al., 2023). Both teachers and learners must work to maximize communication and learning processes. The importance of effective communication is endless in life, learning, and work environments (Muslimin et al., 2023). Ineffective communication is a challenge for clinical learning experiences (De Swardt, 2019). Communication barriers interfere with the learning process (Muslimin et al., 2023). In learning environments, conscious planning should be performed to remove all communication barriers and noises, thus optimizing both communication and learning processes. To review definitions and solutions to communication barriers and noises, please go back to chapters one, two, three, and eight.

In addition, teachers should create a psychologically safe environment so the learners can use their speak up and voice behaviors (Ge, 2020). A psychologically safe environment is a place where people feel free to talk without fear of consequences to their self-image, respect, or career (Edmondson, 1999; Kahn, 1990). In such an environment, the learners will be able to perform otherwise risky behaviors, such as asking for assistance, asking questions, reporting a mistake, speaking up about an idea, and learning from their errors, because they feel that the atmosphere is protected and accepting (Edmondson, 1999; Edmondson et al., 2004; Edmondson & Lei, 2014; Sherman, 2023). The learners will share suggestions without fear of being embarrassed, banned, or punished for mistakes because psychological safety facilitates learning and progress (Edmondson, 1999; Edmondson et al., 2016; Edmondson & Lei, 2014; Remtulla et al., 2021; Sanchez, 2019). Please go back to chapter five for more details about psychological safety.

Interprofessional Education Is Crucial

Today, interprofessional work, collaboration, and teamwork are essential to be able to provide optimal clinical services (Ansa et al., 2020; Diggele et al., 2020; Franklin et al., 2015; Loria, 2024; Rodrigues da Silva et al., 2023; Wang et al., 2022; WHO, 2010). However, most clinicians' education helps them develop the critical knowledge to qualify the young graduate for the practice of their profession (van Diggele et al., 2020; Zheng et al., 2019). Interprofessional education happens when students of two or more different professions learn together, about, and from each other (Loria, 2024; Sindhu, 2023). A collaborative practice (CP) takes place when clinicians of two or more professions work together to benefit patients and the community (Sindhu, 2023). Health professionals need to learn to work as interprofessional team members either during their initial training at their university or while working as clinicians at healthcare organizations.

Interprofessional communication, collaborative practice, and teamwork are difficult for older clinicians, as most of them were not formally trained in interprofessional classrooms. They do not see and feel the need to work collaboratively because they are task- or productivity-oriented. Even today, as science advances, many healthcare education programs choose not to include interprofessional courses in their curriculum due to time constraints—as other new topics are developed, they compete for the time available (O'Keefe & Ward, 2018). Some program leaders may include interprofessional activities (O'Keefe & Ward, 2018) while others think that interprofessional collaboration may come organically to their students during their clinical practices. Attributing value to collaboration and interprofessional work gives students an awareness of how other professions' skills and expertise (Rodrigues da Silva et al., 2023) not only optimize patient outcomes but also health organizational gains.

Strategies to Optimize Communication

We've completed eight chapters of analysis, discovery, and understanding regarding the damaging results of ineffective communication and how optimizing communication will improve outcomes at patient, team, departmental, and organizational levels. The organic process that should follow this learning voyage is the ability to transfer what you've learned to real life. Integrating all the acquired knowledge and applying practical and effective solutions to daily work is the natural step forward. The process to improve communication and collaboration within a healthcare team should include prioritizing communication; understanding the communication cycle and communication styles; removing communication barriers and noises through planning; favoring interprofessional work, teamwork, and collaboration; and promoting psychological safety, power balance, and effective leadership at team and organizational levels.

Assess Your Team

Evaluate your team's preferences and organizational culture. What works best for them? Do your teammates prefer workshops, short meetings, or self-studies using videos, PowerPoint presentations, or Word documents to learn and review topics? Are they always in a hurry? Do they frequently protest when they need to take time from their busy schedules to learn? Do they like to meet and favor fraternization? Think about what has been effective in the past. Short meetings and workshops may promote camaraderie, which in the end will facilitate communication (Guttman et al., 2021).

If you don't know your team's preferences or prefer to bring them into the decision-making process, you can conduct an opinion poll or a survey. You can prepare multiple-choice questions and include open-ended questions asking for their suggestions. Participation by the team members in providing their opinions and ideas can increase their motivation to join the education process.

See the table spanning the following pages. It was by me (the author) with ideas and activities to facilitate the transfer and application of learning to your team and organization.

Table 3

Communication Plan: Applying the Learning

Communication Plan: Applying the Learning		
Steps in a Communication Plan	*Goals: Promote Understanding, Analysis and Practice*	*Learning Application*
Prioritize communication.	Promote knowledge about the importance of communication and the damaging effects of ineffective communication. Educate the team and the organization's leadership.	Prepare and administer different workshops and schedule discussion meetings about communication and its importance. Design a customized workshop. It can be based on ideas from the educational activities in chapters one and two.
Understand the communication cycle and communication styles.	Identify the communication cycle, its elements, and communication styles to facilitate communication among the interprofessional team.	Schedule a meeting or prepare a workshop to educate your team about the communication cycle and elements. Identify each of your communication styles. Give examples. Use educational activities and reflection points as guides for the meeting/workshop.
Remove communication noises.	Identify, analyze, and assess the communication noises that affect your team and decide how to eliminate or minimize them.	Prepare an educational PowerPoint presentation or workshop with definitions and examples of communication noises and how to minimize them. Use chapter two's educational activities as a guide for the process.
Remove communication barriers.	Spot, discuss, and assess the communication barriers that occur among your team members and consider how to eliminate them.	Create a workshop/meeting and invite the team or prepare a PowerPoint or Word document about communication barriers and solutions to distribute to the team. Emphasize those that affect your team. Go back to chapter three for guidance and examples.

Promote psychological safety.	Define psychological safety and consider how to create a positive environment to promote speak up and voice behaviors within the team.	Schedule a team meeting to discuss the meaning of psychological safety, recall examples of it in your daily work together, and perform role-playing activities. Recall situations in which speak up, voice, and silence behaviors were experienced by members of the group. Go back to educational activities in chapter five.
Facilitate power balance.	Explain how to create power balance and how the classic hierarchy interferes with free communication.	Teach your team leaders how to execute open-door policies, a collaborative approach, education, mentoring, a merit-based approach to assigning leadership roles, and activities to improve group dynamics, Go back to chapters six, seven, and eight for methods and guidance.
Effective leadership at the team and organizational levels.	Understand how effective leadership can produce psychological safety.	Design a workshop inviting team leaders to learn about adaptive leadership and how to promote power balance. Go back to chapters five, six, seven, and eight for guidance.
Facilitate interprofessional work through teamwork and collaboration.	Summarize the meanings of interprofessional work, teamwork, and collaboration.	Create various fraternization activities or host Medical Improv workshops to promote camaraderie. Include messages about the importance of interprofessional work, teamwork, and collaboration. Go back to the educational activities in chapters three, four, seven, and eight for guidance.

Educational Activities:
A Personal View of the Author's Learning Journey

This section is an essential part of the learning journey of the book. I am sharing my quest for knowledge and how it has transformed me so I can intentionally join the community of teachers, students, and health professionals who wish to work on their lifelong learning process and optimize their communication skills. We may have other goals such as improving our daily work with our interprofessional teams and ultimately benefiting all the people around us. I have discovered that simple, clear, and unbiased communication has the potential to improve not only our professional endeavors but also our daily lives. I am convinced that by improving communication, we will benefit not only our patients' health and well-being but also our own and that of those around us.

My bumpy ride to discover how to improve communication within interprofessional teams in healthcare started a year and a half ago. As part of my studies for my doctor of education, I identified the necessity of improving communication because my own healthcare team was struggling with it. We had been confronting communication difficulties for years. Our auditors and educators had been providing training and weekly feedback about the correct use of our evaluation tool to assess our patients for months. However, many clinicians were still facing problems using the tool accurately. Finding solutions was imperative because incorrect documentation results in negative findings during internal and external audits. Failing external audits required the agency leadership to take costly remedial actions and lowered the agency quality ratings published for health providers and future patients. Our prestige and the number of referrals decreased.

I was looking for simple and practical solutions. Many colleagues came to me seeking real-world answers because of their confidence in my skills as a teacher. Inspired by their enthusiasm, I began my literature review to gather research for my dissertation and submitted a proposal document to my professors. One of them suggested writing a textbook so I could use my voice to share my research findings, perspective, experiences, and learning process with future readers. I was surprised by her idea but accepted the professor's challenge because I have always believed in my teachers. They have motivated me throughout my life to achieve success and reach my potential.

In the beginning, I thought of communication as a simple and objective process. Someone speaks, and the other person listens and understands the message. The receiver of the message may or may not provide an answer, and the cycle starts again or ends. As I continued my journey, I learned about different beliefs and situations that affect communication. Topics such as trust, psychological safety, power dynamics, attitudes, and perceptions ignited my passion to continue exploring and expanding my perspectives. As I discovered the various communication styles, I identified people who were task-oriented and communicated just because it was part of their work, but they viewed it as an unpleasant, time-consuming part of their jobs. I became more interested in how people's perceptions of and attitudes toward communication affected the process.

I did many interviews, had enlightening discussions, and analyzed communication with many colleagues. I know this quest is going to continue for many years and will lead to other investigations and books. On this voyage, I discovered deeper aspects of communication, such as the need and the desire to interact and communicate, sharing affection, emotions, and experiences not just with the interprofessional team but with people around us. Whether at our jobs or out in the world, communication with patients, family, friends, and strangers is an essential part of being alive.

I am convinced that being skilled communicators will benefit every aspect of our lives, adding value to the effort and energy invested in the process of improving communication. A new goal reached my conscience: to motivate people toward lifelong learning and an understanding of the importance of effective communication, collaboration, and teamwork. I want to encourage people who are not naturally inclined to learn to change their status quo in order to benefit others. This is the final chapter, and the beginning of my next journey toward higher levels of self-awareness and improvement through research. I hope that I inspired you too. Let's keep learning!

Reflective Analysis: Attitudes and Perceptions Scenario

A real-life interprofessional teamwork example will be reviewed to analyze how a health professional can improve their communication processes and accomplish collaboration after simple and clear communication is facilitated. It is the same health professional scenario described and analyzed in chapter one titled "Teresa's Case." Go back to chapter one for the details.

Just to briefly review the case here, Teresa, a physical therapist (PT), called the preadmissions department and used an abrasive tone during a call because they committed a mistake during the intake process that caused her to arrive at the wrong address.

The interprofessional team was called by the clinical manager in confidence to discuss Teresa's abrasive communication practice because it affected their daily teamwork and collaboration processes. The team agreed to work together to promote positive assertive communication and to get her attention when communication was negative or unproductive in the future. If the communication performed by the PT was positive and assertive, the team members agreed to thank her for her positive input. The analysis process will begin using Kolb's Experiential Learning Perspective (Kolb, 1984; McLeod, 2024a). Then, Maslow's Hierarchy of Needs (McLeod, 2024b) will be applied to explain the behaviors.

Improvement of the Communication Process Case Discussion

⇜ Kolb's Learning Perspective Stages ⇝

1) **Concrete Experience**
   Teresa, a PT, was audited by another health professional, a nurse, for a discharge visit and documentation process. Some of the information in the PT evaluation note did not align with other evaluation tools. The auditor, Ana, talked to her about the misalignment of both tools. Ana took photos of both tools and sent them through their company messaging app. The communication process was productive and positive. Throughout this process, Teresa used a tone and wording that was objective, simple, and accurate. Teresa agreed to make the changes and sent them to the auditor successfully. The whole audit resulted in an aligned and correct discharge procedure. It is important to remember that the team had consistently worked together for about three months using positive reinforcement in all the PT's communication processes. The case example discussed is evidence of how using planned teamwork and collaboration resulted in a positive change in communication tone and improved collaboration and audit outcomes.

2) **Reflective Observation**
   The interprofessional team met confidently to work together to promote change in communication behaviors from Teresa, the PT, toward positive and productive processes. The team agreed to use their speak up behavior by working together to promote positive communication and tell her when she showed negative communication processes. They decided that if the communication performed by Teresa was positive and assertive, they would thank her for her positive input verbally. Ana, the auditor, was part of the interprofessional team, and she used positive speak up behavior by asking for what she needed (for the evaluation to be aligned) and

provided evidence (of the misalignment of the evaluation tools) through (photo) documentation. This process of specific speak up behavior helped Teresa see her own mistakes. Teresa responded positively to the auditor's findings and made the corrections without protest using assertive and positive speak up behaviors.

3) **Abstract Conceptualization**
  a. What happened? The team worked together, to provide positive verbal reinforcement, when Teresa's speak up behavior was productive, which resulted in positive communication behavior from Teresa.
  b. What went wrong? The discharge note had some mistakes in documentation, and the different evaluation tools were not aligned. Ana needed to communicate this to Teresa and did so with a call and photo documentation. Communication and collaboration processes occurred positively.
  c. What should they do next time to improve communication and collaboration? Continue good and effective communication, collaboration, and teamwork.
  d. How can they promote positive attitudes and perceptions about communication and collaboration within the team? The team should keep up the good work and celebrate how aligned teamwork can improve the communication tone and purpose of a team member who communicated negatively in the past. The organization should call the clinicians for daily communication huddles; schedule frequent communication workshops for all the staff; and explain the scientific evidence showing that communication, collaboration, and teamwork promote optimal services and outcomes. Clinicians should discuss clinical cases frequently to create a habit of communication and feedback. Team members should be invited to casual team-building activities to facilitate positive attitudes toward and perceptions of communication and collaboration.

4) **Active Experimentation**
The clinicians should apply the learned concepts about communication behaviors: speak up, voice, and silence behaviors. In addition, during small team meetings, you can review psychological safety, positive perceptions and attitudes, and the value of communication and collaboration.

The meetings can be arranged to apply these skills when discussing successful and challenging cases. Each clinician should have the opportunity to practice communication and collaboration skills.

⇜ MASLOW'S HIERARCHY OF NEEDS ⇝

This scenario can be analyzed using the second level of Maslow's Hierarchy of Needs, safety needs, which describes personal security, resources, health, property, and employment (Maslow, 1943; Maslow, 1954; McLeod, 2024b). Every worker values their job security so they can afford all their needs. As the PT, Teresa, noted that the team was aligned in giving her feedback about her communication with them, she became aware of their work together. Since she values her work security, she decided to improve her communication behavior and became aware of the benefits of good communication. Review Figure 3 (pg. 16) for a visual depiction of Maslow's Hierarchy of Needs (McLeod, 2024b).

Every person wants to excel at their job and demonstrate the quality of their performance so they can maintain their employment and fulfill their safety needs. Teresa wanted to be secure in her job and valued receiving positive feedback from her team, so she decided to improve her communication behavior to favor teamwork and collaboration.

Educational Exercises to Perform

This section is an essential part of the learning journey throughout the book. These activities will encourage you to reflect and consider more profound personal experiences. Perform each activity carefully to optimize your communication skills. You can do the activities individually, in pairs, or with your professional team. To assist with the activities, a template was created to be used by the readers as a visual-motor aid when working on communication examples. The template is included in Appendix A.

Role-Playing: Design Scenarios

   a. Invite your team or classmates to do a SWOT analysis to discover your organization's strengths and opportunities (positive) and weaknesses and threats (negative). Then, you can make some decisions about how to start improving your team's communication skills and outcomes (Sharath Kumar & Praveena, 2023).

b. Reflect on the meaning and importance of communication. Think of examples based on your experiences with members of your organization and team. Do you have coworkers who don't like to communicate? Do you have colleagues who interfere with communication and collaboration processes? Create a hypothetical meeting or team discussion to practice positive behaviors and identify negative behaviors during communication processes. Then, consider how to improve communication behaviors within the organization and the team. Go back to Kolb's Experiential Learning Theory to identify and review the behaviors. Recall the experience, reflect on it, analyze it, and practice using what you've learned.

c. Using the table you viewed previously as a guide, create your plan to improve communication in your team and organization. Consider which kinds of activities will be successful for your team culture. Think about ways to facilitate communication, collaboration, psychological safety, and trust within your team. Go back to Kolb's Experiential Learning Theory. Recall the experience, reflect on it, analyze it, and plan for future situations.

d. Create, reflect on, explain, and analyze examples about possible situations that you may encounter in a clinical practice. Explain the benefits of effective communication and how you can make other students, instructors, and clinicians feel comfortable during meetings. Review how Medical Improv workshops, fraternization activities, and daily briefs or huddles would improve communication and trust within your team. Share the evidence-based results of good communication practices. Go back to chapters three, four, and seven for guidance.

Reflection Points

- Think about what you have learned by reading and performing the educational activities in this book. Have you practiced what you've learned? Have you transformed? How?
- Do you like to learn? Are you engaged in your lifelong learning process? Recal theories, concepts, and strategies that you learned when you initially trained as a health professional that are now obsolete. Have you learned new

skills in your profession in the past years that were not available before your graduation?

- Think about communication, teamwork, and collaboration. Explain what each term means to you and give examples of how you participate in them.
- Analyze your interprofessional team. How do you communicate? Is it effective or just minimally functioning? How can you contribute to the improvement of your team's communication process?
- Describe how it feels to work with people with positive and negative perceptions of and attitudes toward communication and teamwork. Recall situations in which you have worked with people with positive or negative attitudes and how they impacted teamwork and outcomes. How can you deal with those attitudes in the future? Give examples.
- Debate, assess, and determine different ways to improve communication and collaboration among your clinical team members or your classmates.
- Are the leaders of your organization open to communication from clinicians, students, and staff? Do they practice an open-door policy?
- Think about ways to improve consideration, understanding, congeniality, and camaraderie among your clinical team members or your classmates.

This is the final chapter; you can return to other chapters' educational activities and case examples to assess your learning process and determine if you would solve the situations differently after reading the whole book. Moreover, you can recall other experiences from your past and start a new analysis. Practice will promote deeper insight and improve your communication skills. Use the template in Appendix A.

Further Reading

1) **Kukko, P., Silén-Lipponen, M., & Saaranen, T.** (2020). *Health care students' perceptions about learning of affective interpersonal communication competence in interprofessional simulations.* Nurse Education Today, 94, 104565. https://doi.org/10.1016/j.nedt.2020.104565.

2) **Ansa, B. E., Zechariah, S., Gates, A. M., Johnson, S. W., Heboyan, V., & De Leo, G.** (2020). *Attitudes and behavior towards interprofessional collaboration among healthcare professionals in a large academic medical center.* Healthcare, 8(3), 323. https://doi.org/10.3390/healthcare8030323.

3) Castañer, X., & Oliveira, N. (2020). *Collaboration, coordination, and cooperation among organizations: Establishing the distinctive meanings of these terms through a systematic literature review.* Journal of Management, 46(6), 965–1001.

4) Guttman, O. T., Lazzara, E. H., Keebler, J. R., Webster, K. L., Gisick, L. M., & Baker, A. L. (2021). D*issecting communication barriers in healthcare: A path to enhancing communication resiliency, reliability, and patient safety.* Journal of Patient Safety, 17(8), e1465-e1471. https://doi.org/10.1097/pts.0000000000000541.

5) Kilag, O. K. T., Malbas, M. H., Miñoza, J. R., Ledesma, M. M. R., Vestal, A. B. E., & Sasan, J. M. V. (2024). *The views of the faculty on the effectiveness of teacher education programs in developing lifelong learning competence.* European Journal of Higher Education and Academic Advancement, 1(2), 92-102. DOI:10.61796/ejheaa.v1i2.106.

6) Muslimin, M., Rusydi, M. A., & Aristya, F. D. (2023). *Intercultural communication barriers of new students in virtual media.* Jurnal Scientia, 12(03), 3052-3057. ISSN 2302-0059.

7) Sindhu, S. (2023). *Interprofessional education and collaborative practice: Need of the hour.* National Journal of Pharmacology and Therapeutics, 1(1), 18-21. https://doi.org/10.4103/NJPT.NJPT_13_23.

8) Loria, K. (2024). *The Importance of Interprofessional Education.* APTA Magazine, 16(2), 36–45. ISSN: 2691-3143.

9) O'Leary, N., Salmon, N., O'Donnell, M., Murphy, S., & Mannion, J. (2023). *Interprofessional education and practice guide: Profiling readiness for practice-based IPE.* Journal of Interprofessional Care, 37(1), 150–155. https://doi.org/10.1080/13561820.2022.2038551.

10) Rodrigues da Silva Noll Gonçalves, J., Noll Gonçalves, R., da Rosa, S. V., Schaia Rocha Orsi, J., Santos de Paula, K. M., Moysés, S. J., & Werneck, R. I. (2023). *Potentialities and limitations of interprofessional education during graduation: A systematic review and thematic synthesis of qualitative studies.* BMC Medical Education, 23(1), 236. https://doi.org/10.1186/s12909-023-04211-6.

11) van Diggele, C., Roberts, C., Burgess, A., & Mellis, C. (2020). *Interprofessional education: Tips for design and implementation.* BMC Medical Education, 20(Suppl 2), 455. https://doi.org/10.1186/s12909-020-02286-z.

12) Zheng, Y. H. E., Palombella, A., Salfi, J., & Wainman, B. (2019). *Dissecting through barriers: A follow-up study on the long-term effects of interprofessional education in a dissection course with healthcare professional students.* Anatomical Sciences Education, 12 (1), 52–60. https://doi.org/10.1002/ase.1791.

BIBLIOGRAPHY

Aase, I. (2016). Interprofessional teamwork training for nursing and medical students in Norway. PhD thesis no. 309. University of Stavanger.

Acton, R. (2019). Mapping the evaluation of problem-oriented pedagogies in higher education: A systematic literature review. Education Sciences, 9(4), Article 269. https://doi.org/10.3390/educsci9040269.

Adamska, K., & Jurek, P. (2017). Adaptation of the four forms of employee silence scale in a Polish sample. Current Issues in Personality Psychology, 5(4), 303-312.https://doi.org/10.5114/cipp.2017.68335.

Agarwal, R., Sands, D. Z., Schneider, J. D., & Smaltz, D. H. (2010). Quantifying the economic impact of communication inefficiencies in US hospitals. Journal of Healthcare Management, 55(4). https://doi.org/10.1097/00115514-201007000-00007.

Alheit, P. (2018). Biographical learning–within the lifelong learning discourse. In Contemporary theories of learning (pp. 153-165). Routledge.

Ansa, B. E., Zechariah, S., Gates, A. M., Johnson, S. W., Heboyan, V., & De Leo, G. (2020). Attitudes and behavior towards interprofessional collaboration among healthcare professionals in a large academic medical center. Healthcare, 8(3), 323. https://doi.org/10.3390/healthcare8030323.

Argote, L., Aven, B. L., & Kush, J. (2018). The effects of communication networks and turnover on transactive memory and group performance. Organization Science, 29(2), 191–206. https://doi.org/10.1287/orsc.2017.1176.

Argyris, C., & Scho¨n, D. (1978). Organizational learning: A theory of action perspective. Addison-Wesley.

Avery, D. R., & Quiñones, M. A. (2002). Disentangling the effects of voice: The incremental roles of opportunity, behavior, and instrumentality in predicting procedural fairness. Journal of Applied Psychology, 87(1), 81–86. https://doi.org/10.1037/0021-9010.87.1.81.

Barnard, R., Jones, J., & Cruice, M. (2020). Communication between therapists and nurses working in inpatient interprofessional teams: Systematic review and meta-ethnography. Disability & Rehabilitation,42(10), 1339–1349. https://doi.org/10.1080/09638288.2018.1526335.

Bates, D. W., Spell, N., Cullen, D. J., Burdick, E., Laird, N., Petersen, L. A., & Leape, L. L.et al. (1997). The costs of adverse drug events in hospitalized patients. JAMA, 277(4), 307-311.https://doi.org/10.1001/jama.1997.03540280045032.

Beer, M. and Eisenstat, R. (2000). 'The silent killers of strategy implementation and learning.' Sloan Management Review, 41, 29–40. https://sloanreview.mit.edu/article/the-silent-killers-of-strategy-implementation-and-learning/.

Berwick, D. M. (2003). Improvement, trust, and the healthcare workforce. Quality and Safety in Health Care, 12(90001), 2i–26. https://doi.org/10.1136/qhc.12.suppl_1.i2.

Biscan, M. P., Milanovic, M., Petrovic, J., & Pale, P. (2021). A review of lecture capture technology and its usage in higher education. 2021 44th International Convention on Information, Communication and Electronic Technology (MIPRO). https://doi.org/10.23919/mipro52101.2021.9597051.

Bligh, M. C., Pearce, C. L., & Kohles, J. C. (2006). The importance of self and shared leadership in team based knowledge work: A meso-level model of leadership dynamics. Journal of Managerial Psychology, 21(4), 296–318. https://doi.org/10.1108/02683940610663105.

Boak, G., Dickens, V., Newson, A., & Brown, L. (2015). Distributed leadership, team working and service improvement in healthcare. Leadership in Health Services, 28(4), 332–344. https://doi.org/10.1108/LHS-02-2015-0001.

Bogart, K., & Stein, N. (1987). Breaking the silence: Sexual harassment in education. Peabody Journal of Education, 64(4), 146–163. https://doi.org/10.1080/01619568709538575.

Boynton, B. [Beth Boynton]. (2022, February 16). Introduction to Medical Improv for Leaders – Reinventing Communication & Culture in Healthcare. [Video] YouTube. https://www.youtube.com/watch?v=u25fw_h4Zvg.

Bridges, Diane, R., Davidson, R. A., Soule Odegard, P., Maki, I. V., & Tomkowiak, J. (2011). Interprofessional collaboration: Three best practice models of interprofessional education. Medical Education Online, 16(1), 6035. https://doi.org/10.3402/meo.v16i0.6035.

Brinsfield, C. T. (2013). Employee silence motives: Investigation of dimensionality and development of measures. Journal of Organizational Behavior, 34(5), 671–697.https://doi.org/10.1002/job.1829.

Busari, J., Moll, F., & Duits, A. (2017). Understanding the impact of interprofessional collaboration on the quality of care: a case report from a small-scale resource limited health care environment. Journal of Multidisciplinary Healthcare, 10, 227–234. https://doi.org/10.2147/jmdh.s140042.

Carney, P. A., Thayer, E. K., Palmer, R., Galper, A. B., Zierler, B., & Eiff, M. P. (2019). The benefits of interprofessional learning and teamwork in primary care ambulatory training settings. Journal of Interprofessional Education & Practice, 15, 119-126. https://doi.org/10.1016/j.xjep.2019.03.011

Carron, A. V., & Brawley, L. R. (2000). Cohesion: Conceptual and measurement issues. Small Group Research, 43(6), 726–743. https://doi.org/10.1177/1046496412468072.

Carver, C. S. (2006). Approach, avoidance, and the self-regulation of affect and action. Motivation and Emotion, 30(2), 105–110. https://doi.org/10.1007/s11031-006-9044-7.

Castañer, X., & Oliveira, N. (2020). Collaboration, coordination, and cooperation among organizations: Establishing the distinctive meanings of these terms through a systematic literature review. Journal of Management, 46(6), 965–1001. https://doi.org/10.1177/0149206320901565.

Chartered Institute of Personnel and Development. (2012). Where has all the trust gone? Stewardship, leadership, and governance. https://www.cipd.org/globalassets/media/knowledge/knowledge-hub/reports/where-has-all-the-trust-gone_2012-sop_tcm18-9644.pdf.

Chen, Y., Yu, C., Yuan, Y., Lu, F., & Shen, W. (2021). The influence of trust on creativity: A review. Frontiers in Psychology, 12, 706234. https://doi.org/10.3389/fpsyg.2021.706234.

Cherry, K. (2023a, March 11). The components of attitude definition, formation, and changes. Verywell Mind. https://www.verywellmind.com/attitudes-how-they-form-change-shape-behavior-2795897.

Cherry, K. (2023b, February 1). What is perception? Recognizing environmental stimuli through the five senses. Verywell Mind. https://www.verywellmind.com/perception-and-the-perceptual-process-2795839.

Connelly, C. E., Zweig, D., Webster, J., & Trougakos, J. P. (2011). Knowledge hiding in organizations. Journal of Organizational Behavior, 33(1), 64–88. https://doi.org/10.1002/job.737De Swardt, H. C. (2019). The clinical environment: A facilitator of professional socialisation. Health SA Gesondheid, 24.1188. https://doi.org/10.4102/hsag.v24i0.1188.

Cortina, L. M., & Magley, V. J. (2003). Raising voice, risking retaliation: Events following interpersonal mistreatment in the workplace. Journal of Occupational Health Psychology, 8(4), 247–265. https://doi.org/10.1037/1076-8998.8.4.247

Crowe, S., Clarke, N., & Brugha, R. (2017). 'You do not cross them': Hierarchy and emotion in doctors' narratives of power relations in specialist training. Social Science & Medicine, 186, 70–77. https://doi.org/10.1016/j.socscimed.2017.05.048 .

de Assis Brito, M., Teixeira Carneiro, C., Rocha Bezerra, M. A., Cardoso Rocha, R., & Santiago da Rocha, S. (2022). Estrategias de comunicación efectivas entre profesionales de la salud en neonatología [Effective communication strategies among health professionals in neonatology]. Infirmarian Global [Global Nursing], 21(3), 548–563. https://doi.org/10.6018/eglobal.502051.

De Maria, W. (2006). Brother secret, sister silence: Sibling conspiracies against managerial integrity. Journal of Business Ethics, 65(3), 219–234. https://doi.org/10.1007/s10551-005-4710-3.

De Stefano, J., Hutman, H., & Gazzola, N. (2017). Putting on the face: A qualitative study of power dynamics in clinical supervision. The Clinical Supervisor, 36(2), 223–240. https://doi.org/10.1080/07325223.2017.1295893.

Dedahanov, A. T., Lee, D., Rhee, J., & Yusupov, S. (2016b). An examination of the associations among cultural dimensions, relational silence, and stress. Personnel Review, 45(3), 593-604. https://doi.org/10.1108/pr-08-2014-0189.

Deeter-Schmelz, D. R., & Norman Kennedy, K. (2003). Patient care teams and customer satisfaction: The role of team cohesion. Journal of Services Marketing, 17(7), 666–684.https://doi.org/10.1108/08876040310501232.

Detert, J. R., & Burris, E. R. (2007). Leadership behavior and employee voice: Is the door really open? Academy of Management Journal, 50(4), 869–884. https://doi.org/10.5465/amj.2007.26279183.

Detert, J. R., & Edmondson, A. C. (2011). Implicit voice theories: Taken-for-granted rules of self-censorship at work. Academy of Management Journal, 54(3), 461–488. https://doi.org/10.5465/amj.2011.61967925.

Dietz, G., & Den Hartog, D. N. (2006). Measuring trust inside organisations. Personnel Review, 35(5), 557–588. https://doi.org/10.1108/00483480610682299.

Dobre, I. (2015). Learning Management Systems for higher education-an overview of available options for higher education organizations. Procedia-Social and Behavioral Sciences, 180, 313-320. https://doi.org/10.1016/j.sbspro.2015.02.122.

Dong, X. T., & Chung, Y. W. (2021). The mediating effect of perceived stress and moderating effect of trust for the relationship between employee silence and behavioral outcomes. Psychological Reports, 124(4), 1715–1737. https://doi.org/10.1177/0033294120942914.

Drescher, M. A., Korsgaard, M. A., Welpe, I. M., Picot, A., & Wigand, R. T. (2014). The dynamics of shared leadership: Building trust and enhancing performance. Journal of Applied Psychology, 99(5), 771–783. https://doi.org/10.1037/a0036474.

Duan, J., Lapointe, É., Xu, Y., & Brooks, S. (2019). Why do employees speak up? Examining the roles of LMX, perceived risk and perceived leader power in predicting voice behavior. Journal of Managerial Psychology, 34(8), 560–572. https://doi.org/10.1108/jmp-11-2018-0534.

Dyne, L. V., Ang, S., & Botero, I. C. (2003). Conceptualizing employee silence and employee voice as multidimensional constructs. Journal of Management Studies, 40(6), 1359–1392. https://doi.org/10.1111/1467-6486.00384.

Edmondson, A. (1999). Psychological safety and learning behavior in work teams. Administrative Science Quarterly, 44(2), 350–383. https://doi.org/10.2307/2666999.

Edmondson, A. C., Higgins, M., Singer, S., & Weiner, J. (2016). Understanding psychological safety in health care and education organizations: A comparative perspective. Research in Human Development, 13(1), 65–83. https://doi.org/10.1080/15427609.2016.1141280.

Edmondson, A. C., Kramer, R. M., & Cook, K. S. (2004). Psychological safety, trust, and learning in organizations: A group-level lens. Trust and distrust in organizations: Dilemmas and Approaches, 12(2004), 239-272. https://doi.org/10.1108/004834805510600083 .

Edmondson, A. C., & Lei, Z. (2014). Psychological safety: The history, renaissance, and future of an interpersonal construct. Annual Review of Organizational Psychology and Organizational Behavior, 1 (1), 23–43. https://doi.org/10.1146/annurev-orgpsych-031413-091305.

Elliot, A. J. (2006). The hierarchical model of approach-avoidance motivation. Motivation and Emotion, 30(2), 111–116. https://doi.org/10.1007/s11031-006-9028-7.

Engum, S. A., & Jeffries, P. R. (2012). Interdisciplinary collisions: Bringing healthcare professionals together. Collegian, 19(3), 145–151. https://doi.org/10.1016/j.colegn.2012.05.005.

Enlow, M., Shanks, L., Guhde, J., & Perkins, M. (2010). Incorporating Interprofessional Communication Skills (ISBARR) into an undergraduate nursing curriculum. Nurse Educator, 35(4), 176–180. https://doi.org/10.1097/nne.0b013e-3181e339ac.

Epstein, N. (2014). Multidisciplinary in-hospital teams improve patient outcomes: A review. Surgical Neurology International, 5(8), 295. https://doi.org/10.4103/2152-7806.139612.

Eriguc, G., Ozer, O., Turac, İ. S., & Songur, C. (2014). Organizational silence among nurses: a study of structural equation modeling. International Journal of Business, Humanities and Technology, 4(1), 150-162. https://www.researchgate.net/publication/269762371_Organizational_Silence_among_Nurses_A_Study_of_Structural_Equation_Modeling.

Eriksen, K. Å., & Heimestøl, S. (2017). Developing a culture of pride, confidence and trust: enhanced collaboration in an interdisciplinary team. International

Practice Development Journal, 7(Suppl), 1–14. https://doi.org/10.19043/ip-dj.7sp.004.

Ernst, F. R., & Grizzle, A. J. (2001). Drug-related morbidity and mortality: Updating the cost-of-illness model. Journal of the American Pharmaceutical Association (1996), 41(2), 192-199. https://doi.org/10.1016/S1086-5802(16)31229-3.

Fan, H.-L., Chang, P.-F., Albanese, D., Wu, J.-J., Yu, M.-J., & Chuang, H.-J. (2016). Multilevel influences of transactive memory systems on individual innovative behavior and team innovation. Thinking Skills and Creativity, 19, 49–59. https://doi.org/10.1016/j.tsc.2015.11.001.

Farrell, D. (1983). Exit, voice, loyalty, and neglect as responses to job dissatisfaction: A multidimensional scaling study. Academy of Management Journal, 26(4), 596–607. https://doi.org/10.5465/255909.

Fast, N. J., Burris, E. R., & Bartel, C. A. (2014). Managing to stay in the dark: Managerial self-efficacy, ego defensiveness, and the aversion to employee voice. Academy of Management Journal, 57(4), 1013–1034. https://doi.org/10.5465/amj.2012.0393.

Fausett, C. M., Korentsides, J. M., Miller, Z. N., & Keebler, J. R. (2024). Adaptive leadership in health care organizations: Five insights to promote effective teamwork. Psychology of Leaders and Leadership, 27(1), 6–26. https://doi.org/10.1037/mgr0000148.

Festinger, L. (1950). Informal social communication. Psychological Review, 57(5), 271–282. https://doi.org/10.1037/h0056932.

Findyartini, A., Kambey, D. R., Yusra, R. Y., Timor, A. B., Khairani, C. D., Setyorini, D., & Soemantri, D. (2019). Interprofessional collaborative practice in primary healthcare settings in Indonesia: A mixed-methods study. Journal of Interprofessional Education & Practice, 17, 100279. https://doi.org/10.1016/j.xjep.2019.100279.

Fleming, P., & Spicer, A. (2003). Working at a cynical distance: Implications for power, subjectivity and resistance. Organization, 10(1), 157–179. https://doi.org/10.1177/1350508403010001376.

Foronda, C., MacWilliams, B., & McArthur, E. (2016). Interprofessional communication in healthcare: An integrative review. Nurse Education in Practice, 19, 36–40. https://doi.org/10.1016/j.nepr.2016.04.005.

Franklin, C. M., Bernhardt, J. M., Lopez, R. P., Long-Middleton, E. R., & Davis, S. (2015). Interprofessional teamwork and collaboration between community health workers and healthcare teams. Health Services Research and Managerial Epidemiology, 2, 233339281557331. https://doi.org/10.1177/2333392815573312.

Frith, L., Sinclair, M., Vehviläinen-Julkunen, K., Beeckman, K., Lotyved, C., & Luybens, A. (2014). Organisational culture in maternity care: a scoping review. Evidence Based Midwifery, 12(1), 16-22. https://pure.ulster.ac.uk/ws/files/12561955/FRITH_et_al_organizational_culture.pdf.

Garfield, S. (2006). 10 reasons why people don't share their knowledge. Knowledge Management Review, 9(2), 10–11. https://www.researchgate.net/profile/Stan-Garfield-2/publication/284397202_10_reasons_why_people_don%27t_share_their_knowledge/links/5f93aa90299bf1b53e407375/10-reasons-why-people-dont-share-their-knowledge.pdf.

Ge, Y. (2020). Psychological safety, employee voice, and work engagement. Social Behavior and Personality: An International Journal, 48 (3). https://doi.org/10.2224/sbp.8907.

Gephart, J. J., Detert, J. R., Treviño, L. K., & Edmondson, A. C. (2009). Silenced by fear: The nature, sources, and consequences of fear at work. Research in Organizational Behavior, 29, 163–193. https://doi.org/10.1016/j.riob.2009.07.002.

Gephart, S. M., & Cholette, M. (2012). Pure communication: A strategy to improve care coordination for high-risk birth. Newborn and Infant Nursing Reviews, 12(2), 109-114. https://doi.org/10.1053/j.nainr.2012.03.007.

Gibson, J. J. (1966). The senses considered as perceptual systems. HoughtonMifflin.

Gibson, J. J. (1972). A theory of direct visual perception. In J. Royce, W. Rozenboom (Eds.), The psychology of knowing (pp. 215 – 240). Gordon & Breach.

Gibson, R., & Singh, J. P. (2004). Wall of silence, the untold story of the medical mistakes that kill and injure millions of Americans. Journal For Healthcare Quality, 26(2), 57. https://doi.org/10.1097/01445442-200403000-00016.

Giroldi, E., Veldhuijzen, W., Dijkman, A., Rozestraten, M., Muris, J., van der Vleuten, C., & van der Weijden, T. (2015). How to gather information from talkative patients in a respectful and efficient manner: a qualitative study of GPs' communication strategies. Family Practice, 33(1), 100–106. https://doi.org/10.1093/fampra/cmv094.

Gladman, T., Gallagher, S., & Grainger, R. (2023). Apps to support learning and professional development in the health professions. Smartphone Apps for Health and Wellness, 177–199. https://doi.org/10.1016/b978-0-323-99271-8.00010-3.

Gladman, T., Tylee, G., Gallagher, S., Mair, J., & Grainger, R. (2021). Measuring the quality of clinical skills mobile apps for student learning: Systematic search, analysis, and comparison of two measurement scales. JMIR MHealth and UHealth, 9(4), e25377. https://doi.org/10.2196/25377.

Gluyas, H. (2015). Effective communication and teamwork promotes patient safety. Nursing Standard, 29(49), 50–57. https://doi.org/10.7748/ns.29.49.50.e10042.

Gorski, T. (2014). Are you talkin'to me? Understand and adapt to different communication styles. The Canadian Manager, 39(1), 22–23..

Grainger, R., Liu, Q., & Gladman, T. (2024). Learning technology in health professions education: Realising an (un) imagined future. Medical Education, 58(1), 36-46.https://doi.org:10.1111/medu.15185.

Grant, A. M. (2013). Rocking the boat but keeping it steady: The role of emotion regulation in employee voice. Academy of Management Journal, 56(6), 1703–1723. https://doi.org/10.5465/amj.2011.0035.

Green, B., Oeppen, R. S., Smith, D. W., & Brennan, P. A. (2017). Challenging hierarchy in healthcare teams – ways to flatten gradients to improve teamwork and patient care. British Journal of Oral and Maxillofacial Surgery, 55(5), 449–453. https://doi.org/10.1016/j.bjoms.2017.02.010.

Gregory, R. (1970). The intelligent eye. Weidenfeld and Nicolson.

Gregory, R. (1974). Concepts and mechanisms of perception. Duckworth.

Gruen, R. (2001). To Err Is Human. Eds. L. T. Kohn, J. M. Corrigan, and M. S. Donaldson. National Academy Press.

Gum, L. F., Prideaux, D., Sweet, L., & Greenhill, J. (2012). From the nurses' station to the health team hub: How can design promote interprofessional collaboration? Journal of Interprofessional Care, 26(1), 21–27. https://doi.org/10.3109/1 3561820.2011.636157.

Guo, L., Decoster, S., Babalola, M. T., De Schutter, L., Garba, O. A., & Riisla, K. (2018). Authoritarian leadership and employee creativity: The moderating role of psychological capital and the mediating role of fear and defensive silence. Journal of Business Research, 92, 219–230. https://doi.org/10.1016/j.jbusres.2018.07.034.

Guttman, O. T., Lazzara, E. H., Keebler, J. R., Webster, K. L., Gisick, L. M., & Baker, A. L. (2021). Dissecting communication barriers in healthcare: A path to enhancing communication resiliency, reliability, and patient safety. Journal of Patient Safety, 17(8), e1465-e1471. https://doi.org/10.1097/ pts.0000000000000541.

Hamilton, A. L., Layden, E. A., Storrar, N., Skinner, J., Harden, J., & Wood, M. (2024). Definition, measurement, precursors, and outcomes of trust within health care teams: A scoping review. Academic Medicine, 99(1), 106–117. https://doi.org/10.1097/acm.0000000000005320.

Hansson, A., Arvemo, T., Marklund, B., Gedda, B., & Mattsson, B. (2010). Working together — primary care doctors' and nurses' attitudes to collaboration. Scandinavian Journal of Public Health, 38(1), 78–85. https://doi.org/10.1177/1403494809347405.

Hao, L., Zhu, H., He, Y., Duan, J., Zhao, T., & Meng, H. (2022). When is silence golden? A meta-analysis on antecedents and outcomes of employee silence. Journal of Business and Psychology, 37(5), 1039–1063. https://doi.org/10.1007/s10869-021-09788-7.

Harmanci Seren, A. K., Topcu, İ., Eskin Bacaksiz, F., Unaldi Baydin, N., Tokgoz Ekici, E., & Yildirim, A. (2018). Organizational silence among nurses and physicians in public hospitals. Journal of Clinical Nursing, 27(7–8), 1440–1451. https://doi.org/10.1111/jocn.14294.

Hart, C. (2015). The elephant in the room: Nursing and nursing power on an interprofessional team. The Journal of Continuing Education in Nursing, 46(8), 349–355.https://doi.org/10.3928/00220124-20150721-15.

Hasfeldt, D., Laerkner, E., & Birkelund, R. (2010). Noise in the Operating Room—What Do We Know? A Review of the Literature. Journal of PeriAnesthesia Nursing, 25(6), 380–386. https://doi.org/10.1016/j.jopan.2010.10.001.

Hazarika, I. (2019). Health workforce governance: Key to the delivery of people-centred care. International Journal of Healthcare Management, 14(2), 358-362. https://doi.org/10.1080/20479700.2019.1647380.

He, H., & Hu, Y. (2021). The dynamic impacts of shared leadership and the transactive memory system on team performance: A longitudinal study. Journal of Business Research, 130, 14–26. https://doi.org/10.1016/j.jbusres.2021.03.007.

Heifetz, R. A., Grashow, A., & Linsky, M. (2009). The practice of adaptive leadership: Tools and tactics for changing your organization and the world. Harvard Business Press.

Hirschman, A. (1970). Exit, voice, and loyalty: responses to decline in firms, organizations, and states. Cambridge: Harvard University Press.

Hobson, J., Talbot, P., Astbury, G., & Mason, T. (2010). Communication. In SAGE Key Concepts series: Key Concepts in Learning Disabilities. Sage UK. Retrieved September 19, 2023, from https://search.credoreference.com/articles/Qm9va0FydGljbGU6MzE2MTIxOA==.

Hogg, M., & Vaughan, G. (2005). Social psychology (4th edition). Prentice-Hall.

Hoonakker, P. L. T., Carayon, P., Walker, J. M., Brown, R. L., & Cartmill, R. S. (2013). The effects of Computerized Provider Order Entry implementation on communication in Intensive Care Units. International Journal of Medical

Informatics, 82(5), e107–e117. https://doi.org/10.1016/j.ijmedinf.2012.11.005.

Hussaini, N., & Varon, J. (2023). Fostering trust in critical care medicine: A comprehensive analysis of patient-provider relationships. Critical Care & Shock, 26(6). ISSN1410-7767.

INACSL, 2016. Standards Committee. INACSL Standards of Best Practice: Simulation Simulation enhanced interprofessional education (sim-IPE). Clinical Simulation in Nursing, 12, 34-38. https://doi.org/10.1016/j.ecns.2016.09.005.

Interprofessional Educational Collaborative. (2016). Core competencies for interprofessional collaboration: 2016 Update. https://www.ipecollaborative.org/assets/2016-Update.pdf.

Jamal, N., Young, V. N., Shapiro, J., Brenner, M. J., & Schmalbach, C. E. (2023). Patient safety/quality improvement primer, part IV: Psychological safety—Drivers to outcomes and wellbeing. Otolaryngology–Head and Neck Surgery, 168(4), 881–888. https://doi.org/10.1177/01945998221126966.

Johnson, J. D. (2016). Interprofessional care teams: the perils of fads and fashions. International Journal of Healthcare Management, 10(2), 127–134. https://doi.org/10.1080/20479700.2016.1268799.

Johnson, J. D. (2019). Network analysis approaches to collaborative information seeking in interprofessional health care teams. Information Research, 24(1). http://InformationR.net/ir/24-1/paper810.html.

Johnson, J., & Bootman, J. (1995). Drug-related morbidity and mortality. A cost of illness model. Archives of Internal Medicine, 155, 1949-1956. https://doi.org/10.1001/archinte.155.18.1949.

Joint Commission. (2022, April). Advancing patient-provider communication and activating Patients. https://www.jointcommission.org/-/media/tjc/newsletters/quick-safety-29-update-3-29-22.pdf.

Joint Commission. (2023). Sentinel Event Data 2022 Annual Review. https://www.jointcommission.org/-/media/tjc/documents/resources/patient-safety-topics/sentinel-event/03162023_sentinel-event-_annual-review_final.pdf.

Kahn, W. A. (1990a). Psychological conditions of personal engagement and disengagement at work. Academy of Management Journal, 33 (4), 692–724. https://doi.org/10.2307/256287.

Kahn, W. A. (1990b). Toward an agenda for business ethics research. Academy of Management Review, 15(2), 311–328. https://doi.org/10.2307/258159.

Kakkar, H., Tangirala, S., Srivastava, N. K., & Kamdar, D. (2016). The dispositional antecedents of promotive and prohibitive voice. Journal of Applied Psychology, 101(9), 1342-1351.https://doi.org/10.1037/apl0000130.

Kao, K.-Y., Hsu, H.-H., Thomas, C. L., Cheng, Y.-C., Lin, M.-T., & Li, H.-F. (2021). Motivating employees to speak up: Linking job autonomy, P-O fit, and employee voice behaviors through work engagement. Current Psychology, 41(11), 7762–7776. https://doi.org/10.1007/s12144-020-01222-0.

Keller, K. B., Eggenberger, T. L., Belkowitz, J., Sarsekeyeva, M., & Zito, A. R. (2013). Implementing successful interprofessional communication opportunities in health care education: A qualitative analysis. International Journal of Medical Education, 4, 253–259. https://doi.org/10.5116/ijme.5290.bca6.

Kilag, O. K. T., Malbas, M. H., Miñoza, J. R., Ledesma, M. M. R., Vestal, A. B. E., & Sasan, J. M. V. (2024). The views of the faculty on the effectiveness of teacher education programs in developing Lifelong Learning Competence. European Journal of Higher Education and Academic Advancement, 1(2), 92-102. https://doi.org/10.61796/ejheaa.v1i2.106.

Kim, J., MacDuffie, J. P., & Pil, F. K. (2010). Employee voice and organizational performance: Team versus representative influence. Human Relations, 63(3), 371–394. https://doi.org/10.1177/0018726709348936.

King's Fund. (2014). Developing collective leadership for health care.https://assets.kingsfund.org.uk/f/256914/x/9406fe95d0/developing_collective_leadership_2014.pdf.

Kish-Gephart, J. J., Detert, J. R., Treviño, L. K., & Edmondson, A. C. (2009). Silenced by fear: The nature, sources, and consequences of fear at work. Research in Organizational Behavior, 29, 163–193. https://doi.org/10.1016/j.riob.2009.07.002.

Klammer, J., Skarlicki, D. P., & Barclay, L. (2002). Speaking up in the Canadian military: The roles of voice, being heard, and generation in predicting civic virtue. Canadian Journal of Behavioural Science / Revue Canadienne Des Sciences Du Comportement, 34(2), 122–130. https://doi.org/10.1037/h0087162.

Knoll, M., Hall, R. J., & Weigelt, O. (2019). A longitudinal study of the relationships between four differentially motivated forms of employee silence and burnout. Journal of Occupational Health Psychology, 24(5), 572–589. https://doi.org/10.1037/ocp0000143.

Knoll, M., & Redman, T. (2016). Does the Presence of voice imply the absence of silence? The Necessity to Consider Employees' Affective Attachment and Job Engagement. Human Resource Management, 55(5), 829–844. https://doi.org/10.1002/hrm.21744.

Knoll, M., & van Dick, R. (2013). Do I hear the whistle…? A first attempt to measure four forms of employee silence and their correlates. Journal of Business Ethics, 113(2), 349–362. https://doi.org/10.1007/s10551-012-1308-4.

Kohn, L., Corrigan, J., & Donaldson, M. (1999). To err is human: Building a safer health system. Washington, DC: National Academy Press.

Kolb, D. A. (1984). Experiential learning: Experience as the source of learning and Development. Prentice-Hall.

Kovič, D., & McMahon, A. (2023). Building trust: supervisees' experience of power dynamics in transdisciplinary workplace supervision. Journal of Social Work Practice, 37(4), 403–417. https://doi.org/10.1080/02650533.2022.2162491.

Kukko, P., Silén-Lipponen, M., & Saaranen, T. (2020). Health care students' perceptions about learning of affective interpersonal communication competence in interprofessional simulations. Nurse Education Today, 94, 104565. https://doi.org/10.1016/j.nedt.2020.104565.

Kukora, S. K., Batell, B., Umoren, R., Gray, M. M., Ravi, N., Thompson, C., & Zikmund-Fisher, B. J. (2020). Hilariously bad news: Medical Improv as a novel approach to teach communication skills for bad news disclosure. Academic Pediatrics, 20(6), 879–881. https://doi.org/10.1016/j.acap.2020.05.003.

Kyaw, B. M., Saxena, N., Posadzki, P., Vseteckova, J., Nikolaou, C. K., George, P. P., Divakar, U., Masiello, I., Kononowicz, A. A., Zary, N., & Tudor Car, L. (2019). Virtual reality for health professions education: Systematic review and meta-analysis by the Digital Health Education Collaboration. Journal of Medical Internet Research, 21(1), e12959. https://doi.org/10.2196/12959.

Laatikainen, O., Sneck, S., & Turpeinen, M. (2022). Medication-related adverse events in health care—what have we learned? A narrative overview of the current knowledge. European Journal of Clinical Pharmacology, 1-12. https://doi.org/10.1007/s00228-021-03213-x.

Labrague, L. J., Lorica, J., Nwafor, C. E., Bogaert, P., & Cummings, G. G. (2020). Development and psychometric testing of the toxic leadership behaviors of nurse managers (ToxBH NM) scale. Journal of Nursing Management, 28(4), 840–850. Portico. https://doi.org/10.1111/jonm.13008.

Labrague, L. J., McEnroe-Petitte, D. M., Papathanasiou, I. V., Edet, O. B., Tsaras, K., Leocadio, M. C., Colet, P., Kleisiaris, C. F., Fradelos, E. C., Rosales, R. A., Vera Santos-Lucas, K., & Velacaria, P. I. T. (2018). Stress and coping strategies among nursing students: an international study. Journal of mental health (Abingdon, England), 27(5), 402–408. https://doi.org/10.1080/09638237.2017.1417552.

Lee, M., Ong, Y. H., & Martimianakis, M. A. (2022). Ideological dilemmas of healthcare professionals who do not speak up at interprofessional team meetings. Journal of Interprofessional Care, 37(1), 1–10. https://doi.org/10.1080/135

61820.2022.2037530.

LePine, J. A., & Van Dyne, L. (1998). Predicting voice behavior in work groups. Journal of Applied Psychology, 83(6), 853–868. https://doi.org/10.1037/0021-9010.83.6.853.

Lewis, K. (2003). Measuring transactive memory systems in the field: Scale development and validation. Journal of Applied Psychology, 88(4), 587–604. https://doi.org/10.1037/0021-9010.88.4.587.

Lewis, K., Lange, D., & Gillis, L. (2005). Trans.active memory systems, learning, and learning transfer. Organization Science, 16(6), 581–598. https://doi.org/10.1287/orsc.1050.0143.

Lingard, L. (2004). Communication failures in the operating room: an observational classification of recurrent types and effects. Quality and Safety in Health Care, 13(5), 330–334. https://doi.org/10.1136/qshc.2003.008425.

Lloyd, V. J., Schneider, J., Scales, K., Bailey, S., & Jones, R. (2011). Ingroup identity as an obstacle to effective multiprofessional and interprofessional teamwork: findings from an ethnographic study of healthcare assistants in dementia care. Journal of Interprofessional Care, 25(5), 345–351. https://doi.org/10.3109/1356 1820.2011.567381.

Loria, K. (2024). The Importance of Interprofessional Education. APTA Magazine, 16(2), 36–45. ISSN: 2691-3143.

Lott, A. J., & Lott, B. E. (1965). Group cohesiveness as interpersonal attraction: A review of relationships with antecedent and consequent variables. Psychological Bulletin, 64(4), 259–309. https://doi.org/10.1037/h0022386.

Luetsch, K., & Scuderi, C. (2020). Experiences of medical dominance in pharmacist-doctor interactions-An elephant in the room?. Research in Social and Administrative Pharmacy, 16(9), 1177-1182. https://doi.org/10.1016/j.sapharm.2019.12.013.

Lyndon, A., Sexton, J. B., Simpson, K. R., Rosenstein, A., Lee, K. A., & Wachter, R. M. (2011). Predictors of likelihood of speaking up about safety concerns in labour and delivery. BMJ Quality & Safety, 21(9), 791–799. https://doi.org/10.1136/bmjqs-2010-050211.

MacDonald, D. K. C. (2006). Noise and fluctuations: An introduction. Courier Corporation. Shannon, C.E. Communication in the presence of noise.

Madrid, H. P., Patterson, M. G., & Leiva, P. I. (2015). Negative core affect and employee silence: How differences in activation, cognitive rumination, and problem-solving demands matter. Journal of Applied Psychology, 100(6), 1887–1898. https://doi.org/10.1037/a0039380.

Mahon, A., & Brookes, S. L. S. (Ed.) (2013). Relationships in healthcare: trust in transition? In Trust and Confidence in Government and Public Services (1st ed.). Routledge.

Mao, C., Chang, C.-H., Johnson, R. E., & Sun, J. (2019). Incivility and employee performance, citizenship, and counterproductive behaviors: Implications of the social context. Journal of Occupational Health Psychology, 24(2), 213–227. https://doi.org/10.1037/ocp0000108.

Maqbool, S., Černe, M., & Bortoluzzi, G. (2019). Micro-foundations of innovation. European Journal of Innovation Management, 22(1), 125–145. https://doi.org/10.1108/ejim-01-2018-0013.

Maslow, A. H. (1943). A theory of human motivation. Psychological Review, 50(4), 370–396. https://doi.org/10.1037/h0054346.

Maslow, A. H. (1954). Motivation and personality. Harper and Row.

Mayer, R. C., Davis, J. H., & Schoorman, F. D. (2006). An integrative model of organizational trust. Organizational Trust, 82–108. https://doi.org/10.1093/oso/9780199288496.003.0004.

McDonald, J., Jayasuriya, R., & Harris, M. F. (2012). The influence of power dynamics and trust on multidisciplinary collaboration: a qualitative case study of type 2 diabetes mellitus. BMC Health Services Research, 12(1). https://doi.org/10.1186/1472-6963-12-63.

McClean, E. J., Burris, E. R., & Detert, J. R. (2013). When does voice lead to exit? It Depends on Leadership. Academy of Management Journal, 56(2), 525–548. https://doi.org/10.5465/amj.2011.0041.

McLean, L. D. (2005). Organizational culture's influence on creativity and innovation: A review of the literature and implications for human resource development. Advances in Developing Human Resources, 7(2), 226–246. https://doi.org/10.1177/1523422305274528.

McLeod, S. (2023, June 13). Components of Attitude: ABC Model. Simply Psychology. https://www.simplypsychology.org/attitudes.html.

McLeod, S. (2024a, February 2). Kolb's learning styles and experiential learning cycle. Simply Psychology. https://www.simplypsychology.org/learning-kolb.html.

McLeod, S. (2024b, January 24). Maslow's Hierarchy of Needs. Simply Psychology. https://www.simplypsychology.org/maslow.html.

Mehta, A., Fu, B., Chou, E., Mitchell, S., & Fessell, D. (2020). Improv: Transforming physicians and medicine. Medical Science Educator, 31(1), 263–266. https://doi.org/10.1007/s40670-020-01174-x.

Meyer, S. & Ward, P. (2008). Do your patients trust you? A sociological understanding of the implications of patient mistrust in healthcare professionals. Australasian Medical Journal, 1(1). https://doi.org/10.4066/amj.2008.7.

Mickan, S. M., & Rodger, S. A. (2005). Effective health care teams: A model of six characteristics developed from shared perceptions. Journal of Interprofessional Care, 19(4), 358–370.https://doi.org/10.1080/13561820500165142.

Miller, A. (1993). Breaking down the wall of silence: The liberating experience of facing painful truth. New York: Meridian.

Milliken, F. J., & Morrison, E. W. (2003). Shades of Silence: Emerging Themes and Future Directions for Research on Silence in Organizations. Journal of Management Studies, 40(6), 1563–1568. https://doi.org/10.1111/1467-6486.00391.

Milliken, F. J., Morrison, E. W., & Hewlin, P. F. (2003). An exploratory study of employee silence: Issues that employees don't communicate upward and why. Journal of Management Studies, 40(6), 1453–1476. https://doi.org/10.1111/1467-6486.00387.

Mollen Commission. (1994). Commission to Investigate Allegations of Police Corruption and the Anti-Corruption Procedures of the Police Department Report (The City of New York, New York).

Morrison, E. W. (2011). Employee voice behavior: Integration and directions for future research. Academy of Management Annals, 5(1), 373–412. https://doi.org/10.5465/19416520.2011.574506.

Morrison, E. W., & Milliken, F. J. (2000). Organizational silence: A barrier to change and development in a pluralistic world. Academy of Management Review, 25(4), 706–725. https://doi.org/10.5465/amr.2000.3707697.

Morrison, E. W., See, K. E., & Pan, C. (2014). An Approach Inhibition Model of employee silence: The joint effects of personal sense of power and target openness. Personnel Psychology, 68(3), 547–580. https://doi.org/10.1111/peps.12087.

Mueller, C. A., Tetzlaff, B., Theile, G., Fleischmann, N., Cavazzini, C., Geister, C., Scherer, M., Weyerer, S., van den Bussche, H., & Hummers Pradier, E. (2014). Interprofessional collaboration and communication in nursing homes: a qualitative exploration of problems in medical care for nursing home residents – study protocol. Journal of Advanced Nursing, 71(2), 451–457. https://doi.org/10.1111/jan.12545.

Muslimin, M., Rusydi, M. A., & Aristya, F. D. (2023). Intercultural communication barriers of new students in virtual media. Jurnal Scientia, 12(03), 3052-3057. ISSN 2302-0059.

Narasimhan, A. (2023). Raising vital voices in the boardroom: Group dynamics can stop members Speaking out, so how do we empower them? By Anand Narasimhan. Financial Times, 21-23. https://www.ft.com/content/99e17420-2628-43ba-b6f4-e9cc25d48e9b.

Narayan, M. C. (2013). Using SBAR Communications in Efforts to Prevent Patient Rehospitalizations. Home Healthcare Nurse, 31(9), 504–515. https://doi.org/10.1097/nhh.0b013e3182a87711.

Nester, J. (2016). The importance of interprofessional practice and education in the era of accountable care. North Carolina Medical Journal, 77(2), 128–132. https://doi.org/10.18043/ncm.77.2.128.

Nikolaou, I., Vakola, M., & Bourantas, D. (2011). The role of silence on employees' attitudes "the day after" a merger. Personnel Review, 40(6), 723–741. https://doi.org/10.1108/00483481111169652.

Nimmon, L., & Stenfors-Hayes, T. (2016). The "Handling" of power in the physician-patient encounter: Perceptions from experienced physicians. BMC Medical Education, 16(1). https://doi.org/10.1186/s12909-016-0634-0.

Noyes, A. L. (2022). Navigating the Hierarchy: Communicating Power Relationships in Collaborative Health Care Groups. Management Communication Quarterly, 36(1), 62–91. https://doi.org/10.1177/08933189211025737.

Nyberg, D. (1993). The Varnished Truth: Truth-telling and Deceiving in Ordinary Life. Chicago: University of Chicago.

O'Brien, D., Butler, M. M., & Casey, M. (2021). The importance of nurturing trusting relationships to embed shared decision-making during pregnancy and childbirth. Midwifery, 98, 102987. https://doi.org/10.1016/j.midw.2021.102987.

O'Donovan, R., & McAuliffe, E. (2020a). A systematic review exploring the content and outcomes of interventions to improve psychological safety, speaking up and voice behaviour. BMC Health Services Research, 20(1). https://doi.org/10.1186/s12913-020-4931-2.

O'Donovan, R., & McAuliffe, E. (2020b). Exploring psychological safety in healthcare teams to inform the development of interventions: Combining observational, survey and interview data. BMC Health Services Research, 20(1), Article 810. https://doi.org/10.1186/s12913-020-05646-z .

O'Keefe, M., & Ward, H. (2018). Implementing interprofessional learning curriculum: How problems might also be answers. BMC Medical Education, 18(1). https://doi.org/10.1186/s12909-018-1231-1.

Okpala, P. (2017). Harnessing the power of collaborative leadership in the management of chronic health conditions. International Journal of Healthcare Management, 12(4), 302–307. https://doi.org/10.1080/20479700.2017.1414109.

Okpala, P. (2021). Addressing power dynamics in interprofessional health care teams. International Journal of Healthcare Management, 14(4), 1326–1332. https://doi.org/10.1080/20479700.2020.1758894.

O'Leary, N., Salmon, N., O'Donnell, M., Murphy, S., & Mannion, J. (2023). Interprofessional education and practice guide: Profiling readiness for practice-based IPE. Journal of Interprofessional Care, 37(1), 150–155. https://doi.org/10.1080/13561820.2022.2038551.

O'Reilly III, C. A. (1982). Variations in decision makers' use of information sources: The impact of quality and accessibility of information. Academy of Management Journal, 25(4), 756-771. https://doi.org/10.5465/256097.

Organ, D. W. (1988). Organizational citizenship behavior: The"good soldier" syndrome. Lexington, MA: Lexington Books.

Pack, R., Columbus, L., Duncliffe, T. H., Banner, H., Singh, P., Seemann, N., & Taylor, T. (2022). "Maybe I'm not that approachable": using simulation to elicit team leaders' perceptions of their role in facilitating speaking up behaviors. Advances in Simulation, 7(1), 31. https://doi.org/10.1186/s41077-022-00227-y.

Perlow, L., & Williams, S. (2003). Is silence killing your company? IEEE Engineering Management Review, 31(4), 18–18. https://doi.org/10.1109/emr.2003.24935.

Piaget, J. (1953). Logic and Psychology. Manchester: Manchester University Press.

Pinder, C. C., & Harlos, K. P. (2001). Employee silence: Quiescence and acquiescence as responses to perceived injustice. Research in Personnel and Human Resources Management, 20, 331–369. https://doi.org/10.1016/s0742-7301(01)20007-3.

Prichard, J. S., & Ashleigh, M. J. (2007). The effects of team-skills training on transactive memory and performance. Small Group Research, 38(6), 696–726. https://doi.org/10.1177/1046496407304923.

Prouska, R., & Psychogios, A. (2016). Do not say a word! Conceptualizing employee silence in a long-term crisis context. The International Journal of Human Resource Management, 29(5), 885–914. https://doi.org/10.1080/09585192.2016.1212913.

Rabøl, L. I., Andersen, M. L., Østergaard, D., Bjørn, B., Lilja, B., & Mogensen, T. (2011). Descriptions of verbal communication errors between staff. An analysis of 84 root cause analysis-reports from Danish hospitals. BMJ quality & safety, 20(3), 268-274. http://doi:10.1136/bmjqs.2010.040238.

Reeves, S., Fletcher, S., Barr, H., Birch, I., Boet, S., Davies, N., McFadyen, A., Rivera, J., & Kitto, S. (2016). A BEME systematic review of the effects of interprofessional education: BEME Guide No. 39. Medical Teacher, 38(7), 656–668. https://doi.org/10.3109/0142159X.2016.1173663.

Reeves, S., Pelone, F., Harrison, R., Goldman, J., & Zwarenstein, M. (2017, June 22). Interprofessional collaboration to improve professional practice and healthcare outcomes. The Cochrane Database of Systematic Reviews, 6(6), CD000072. http://europepmc.org/abstract/MED/28639262.

Remtulla, R., Hagana, A., Houbby, N., Ruparell, K., Aojula, N., Menon, A., Thavarajasingam, S. G., & Meyer, E. (2021). Exploring the barriers and facilitators of psychological safety in primary care teams: a qualitative study. BMC Health Services Research, 21(1). https://doi.org/10.1186/s12913-021-06232-7.

Roberts, F. E., & Goodhand, K. (2018). Scottish healthcare student's perceptions of an interprofessional ward simulation: An exploratory, descriptive study. Nursing & Health Sciences, 20(1), 107–115. https://doi.org/10.1111/nhs.12393.

Rodrigues da Silva Noll Gonçalves, J., Noll Gonçalves, R., da Rosa, S. V., Schaia Rocha Orsi, J., Santos de Paula, K. M., Moysés, S. J., & Werneck, R. I. (2023). Potentialities and limitations of Interprofessional education during graduation: A systematic review and thematic synthesis of qualitative studies. BMC Medical Education, 23(1), 236. https://doi.org/10.1186/s12909-023-04211-6.

Rogers, L., Hughes Spence, S., Aivalli, P., De Brún, A., & McAuliffe, E. (2024). A systematic review critically appraising quantitative survey measures assessing power dynamics among multidisciplinary teams in acute care settings. Journal of Interprofessional Care, 38(1), 156–171. https://doi.org/10.1080/13561820.2023.2168632.

Rosen, S., & Tesser, A. (1970). On reluctance to communicate undesirable information: The MUM effect. Sociometry, 33(3), 253. https://doi.org/10.2307/2786156.

Ross, H., Tod, A. M., & Clarke, A. (2015). Understanding and achieving person centred care: The nurse perspective. Journal of Clinical Nursing, 24(9-10), 1223-1233. https://doi.org/10.1111/jocn.12662.

Roter, A.B. (2017). Understanding and Recognizing Dysfunctional Leadership: The Impact of Dysfunctional Leadership on Organizations and Followers (1st ed.). Routledge. https://doi.org/10.4324/9781315549286.

Rothwell, G. R., & Baldwin, J. N. (2007). Ethical Climate Theory, whistle-blowing, and the code of Silence in police agencies in the state of Georgia. Journal of Business Ethics, 70(4), 341–361. https://doi.org/10.1007/s10551-006-9114-5.

Royse, L., Nolan, N., & Hoffman, K. (2020). Using a sociogram to characterize communication during an interprofessional team huddle. Journal of Multidisciplinary Healthcare, 1583-1593. https://doi.org/10.2147/jmdh.s273746.

Ryan, K. D. and Oestreich, D. K. (1991). Driving Fear Out of the Workplace: How to Overcome the Invisible Barriers to Quality, Productivity, and Innovation. San Francisco: Jossey-Bass.

Salas, E., Shuffler, M. L., Thayer, A. L., Bedwell, W. L., & Lazzara, E. H. (2014). Understanding and Improving Teamwork in Organizations: A Scientifically Based Practical Guide. Human Resource Management, 54(4), 599–622. Portico. https://doi.org/10.1002/hrm.21628.

Sanchez, E. C. (2019). The effect of servant leadership on healthcare employee psychological safety and employee behaviours that lead to job thriving and performance (Master's thesis, University of Twente).

Sanko, J. S. (2015). Exploring the cohesion—performance relationship in inter-professional healthcare teams (Publication No. 1687760317) [PhD dissertations, University of Miami].ProQuest One Academic. https://scholarship.miami.edu/esploro/outputs/doctoral/Exploring-the-Cohesion-Performance-Relationship-in-Inter-professional/991031447944702976.

Sasan, J. M., & Baritua, J. C. (2022). Distance learning as a learning modality for education during the COVID-19 pandemic. Science and Education, 3(8), 35-44. https://doi.org/10.2478/rem-2022-0004.

Schneider, C., Anders, P., & Rotthoff, T. (2024). "It is great what we have learned from each other!"–Bedside teaching in interprofessional small groups using the example of Parkinson's disease. GMS Journal for Medical Education, 41(1). ISSN 2366-5017.

Sergy, L. (2017). What is communication? In Handy Answer: The Handy Communication Answer Book. Visible Ink Press. Retrieved September 18, 2023, from https://search.credoreference.com/es/articles/Qm9va0FydGljbGU6NDMyMzQyMg==.

Sharath Kumar, C.R. & Praveena, K.B. (2023). SWOT analysis. International Journal of Advanced Research, 11(09), 744-748. 10.21474/IJAR01/17584.

Sharkiya, S. (2023). Type of article: Quality communication can improve patient-centred health outcomes among older patients: A systematic review. https://doi.org/10.21203/rs.3.rs-2789752/v1.

Sherf, E. N., Parke, M. R., & Isaakyan, S. (2021). Distinguishing voice and silence at work: Unique relationships with perceived impact, psychological safety, and burnout. Academy of Management Journal, 64(1), 114–148.https://doi.org/10.5465/amj.2018.1428.

Sherf, E. N., Tangirala, S., & Venkataramani, V. (2019). Why managers do not seek voice from Employees: The importance of managers' personal control and long-term orientation. Organization Science, 30(3), 447–466.https://doi.org/10.1287/orsc.2018.1273.

Sherman, R. O. (2023). Creating psychological safety so nurses speak up and speak out. The Ohio Nurses Association's Code Red Campaign: Advocating for Safe Staffing Laws in Ohio, 5.

Sindhu, S. (2023). Interprofessional education and collaborative practice: Need of the hour. National Journal of Pharmacology and Therapeutics, 1(1), 18-21. 10.4103/NJPT.NJPT_13_23.

Sinek, S. (2014, March). Why good leaders make you feel safe. [Video] TED Conferences. https://video.search.yahoo.com/search/video?fr=mca-fee&p=why+good+leaders+make+you+feel+safe+from+ted+2014+by+si-mon+sinek+on+march+2014&type=E210US1500G0#id=1&vid=4e8467464e-8815a85f7adcfdc4f9cc2e&action=click.

Spaulding, E. M., Marvel, F. A., Jacob, E., Rahman, A., Hansen, B. R., Hanyok, L. A., Martin, S. S., & Han, H.-R. (2019). Interprofessional education and collaboration among healthcare students and professionals: A systematic review and call for action. Journal of Interprofessional Care, 1–10. https://doi.org/10.1080/13561820.2019.1697214.

Spitzberg, B.H., Cupach, W.R., 2011. Interpersonal skills. In: Knapp, M.L., Daly, J.A. (Eds), The Sage Handbook of Interpersonal Communication. Sage Publications, Thousand Oaks, pp. 481–524.

Srivastava, S., Jain, A. K., & Sullivan, S. (2019). Employee silence and burnout in India: The mediating role of emotional intelligence. Personnel Review, 48(4), 1045–1060. https://doi.org/10.1108/pr-03-2018-0104.

Stevens, M., Rees, T., & Cruwys, T. (2021). Social identity leadership in sport and exercise: Current status and future directions. Psychology of Sport and Exercise, 55, Article 101931.https://doi.org/10.1016/j.psychsport.2021.101931.

Steward, E. (2023). Interprofessional team trust in maternity services: a service evaluation. British Journal of Midwifery, 31(3), 126–132.https://doi.org/10.12968/bjom.2023.31.3.126.

Stray, K., Wibe, T., Debesay, J., & Bye, A. (2024). Older adults' perceptions and experiences of interprofessional communication as part of the delivery of integrated care in the primary healthcare sector: a meta-ethnography of qualitative studies. BMC Geriatrics, 24(1). https://doi.org/10.1186/s12877-024-04745-4.

Tanco, K., Rhondali, W., Park, M., Liu, D., & Bruera, E. (2016). Predictors of trust in the medical profession among cancer patients receiving palliative care: A preliminary study. Journal of Palliative Medicine, 19(9), 991–994. https://doi.org/10.1089/jpm.2016.0089.

Tang, C. J., Chan, S. W., Zhou, W. T., & Liaw, S. Y. (2013). Collaboration between hospital physicians and nurses: An integrated literature review. International Nursing Review, 60(3), 291–302. Portico. https://doi.org/10.1111/inr.12034.

Tannenbaum, S., & Salas, E. (2020). Teams that work: The seven drivers of team effectiveness. Oxford University Press.

Taplin, S. H., Foster, M. K., & Shortell, S. M. (2013). Organizational Leadership For Building Effective Health Care Teams. The Annals of Family Medicine, 11(3), 279–281. https://doi.org/10.1370/afm.1506.

Thomas, C. M., Bertram, E., & Johnson, D. (2009). The SBAR communication technique. Nurse Educator, 34(4), 176–180. https://doi.org/10.1097/nne.0b013e3181aaba54.

Thomas, C. M., McIntosh, C. E., Lamar, R. A., & Allen, R. L. (2017). Sleep deprivation in nursing students: The negative impact for quality and safety. Journal of Nursing Education and Practice, 7(5), 87. https://doi.org/10.5430/jnep.v7n5p87.

Tolle, S. L., Vernon, M. M., McCombs, G., & De Leo, G. (2019). Interprofessional education in dental hygiene: Attitudes, barriers and practices of program faculty. American Dental Hygienists' Association, 93(2), 13-22. https://jdh.adha.org/content/93/2/13.full.

Torralba, K. D., Jose, D., & Byrne, J. (2020). Psychological safety, the hidden curriculum, and ambiguity in medicine. Clinical Rheumatology, 39(3), 667–671. https://doi.org/10.1007/s10067-019-04889-4.

Trautman, N. E. (2001). Police code of silence: Facts revealed. Law and Order Magazine, 49, 68–76.

Tsarouha, E., Stuber, F., Seifried-Dübon, T., Radionova, N., Schnalzer, S., Nikendei, C., Genrich, M., Worringer, B., Stiawa, M., Mulfinger, N., Gündel, H., Junne, F., & Rieger, M. A. (2021). Reflection on leadership behavior: Potentials and limits in the implementation of stress-preventive leadership of middle management in hospitals—A qualitative evaluation of a participatory developed intervention. Journal of Occupational Medicine and Toxicology, 16 (1), Article 51. https://doi.org/10.1186/s12995-021-00339-7.

Tullock, G., & Hirschman, A. O. (1970). Exit, voice and loyalty: Responses to decline in firms, organizations, and states. The Journal of Finance, 25(5), 1194. https://doi.org/10.2307/2325604.

Umphress, E. E., & Bingham, J. B. (2011). When employees do bad things for good reasons: Examining unethical pro-organizational behaviors. Organization Science, 22(3), 621–640. https://doi.org/10.1287/orsc.1100.0559.

van Diggele, C., Roberts, C., Burgess, A., & Mellis, C. (2020). Interprofessional education: Tips for design and implementation. BMC Medical Education, 20(Suppl 2), 455. https://doi.org/10.1186/s12909-020-02286-z.

van Dyne, L., Ang, S., & Botero, I. C. (2003). Conceptualizing employee silence and employee voice as multidimensional constructs. Journal of Management Studies, 40(6), 1359–1392. https://doi.org/10.1111/1467-6486.00384.

van Lamoen, M. A. S., Cloodt, M., & Alblas, A. A. (2023). Collaborative innovation in a military organization: The importance of transactive memory, knowledge sharing, and learning from failure. IEEE Transactions on Engineering Management. Advance online publication. https://doi.org/10.1109/TEM.2023.3269851.

VanVactor, J. D. (2010). Health care logistics response in a disaster. Journal of Homeland Security and Emergency Management, 7(1). https://doi.org/10.2202/1547-7355.1725.

Vardell, E., & Nelson, S. B. (2022). Teaching reference interview skills with Improv. Journal of Education for Library and Information Science, 63(1), 38–56. https://doi.org/10.3138/jelis-2020-0098.

Velásquez, S. T., Ferguson, D., Lemke, K. C., Bland, L., Ajtai, R., Amezaga, B., Cleveland, J., Ford, L. A., Lopez, E., Richardson, W., Saenz, D., & Zorek, J. A. (2022). Interprofessional communication in medical simulation: Findings from a scoping review and implications for academic medicine. BMC Medical Education, 22(1), 204. https://doi.org/10.1186/s12909-022-03226-9.

Velentzas, J. O. H. N., & Broni, G. (2014). Communication cycle: Definition, process, models and examples. Recent Advances in Financial Planning and Product Development, 17, 117-131. ISBN: 978-1-61804-261-3.

Velji, K., Baker, G., Fancott, C., Andreoli, A., Boaro, N., Tardif, G., Aimone, E., & Sinclair, L. (2008). Effectiveness of an adapted SBAR communication tool for a rehabilitation setting. Healthcare Quarterly, 11(sp), 72–79. https://doi.org/10.12927/hcq.2008.19653.

Viberg, O., Hatakka, M., Bälter, O., & Mavroudi, A. (2018). The current landscape of learning analytics in higher education. Computers in Human Behavior, 89, 98–110. https://doi.org/10.1016/j.chb.2018.07.027.

Wagner, E. H. (2000). The role of patient care teams in chronic disease management. BMJ, 320(7234), 569–572. https://doi.org/10.1136/bmj.320.7234.569.

Walker, J., & Hirsch, B. (2020). Promoting interdisciplinary communication as a vital function of effective teamwork to positively impact patient outcomes, satisfaction, and employee engagement. Journal of Medical Imaging and Radiation Sciences, 51(4), S107-S111.https://doi.org/10.1016/j.jmir.2020.07.002.

Wang, A.-C., Hsieh, H.-H., Tsai, C.-Y., & Cheng, B.-S. (2012). Does value congruence lead to voice? Cooperative voice and cooperative silence under team and differentiated transformational leadership. Management and Organization Review, 8(2), 341–370. https://doi.org/10.1111/j.1740-8784.2011.00255.x.

Wang, W., Liang, Z., Blazeck, A., & Greene, B. (2015). Improving Chinese nursing students' communication skills by utilizing video-stimulated recall and role-play case scenarios to introduce them to the SBAR technique. Nurse Education Today, 35(7), 881–887. https://doi.org/10.1016/j.nedt.2015.02.010

Wang, W., Shen, J., Greene, W. B., Ren, D., & Sherwood, P. (2022). The effect of ISBARR on knowledge of and attitudes about interprofessional communication skills among Chinese undergraduate nursing students. Nurse Education Today, 109, 105207. https://doi.org/10.1016/j.nedt.2021.105207.

Watson, K., & Fu, B. (2016). Medical Improv: A novel approach to teaching communication and professionalism skills. Annals of Internal Medicine, 165(8), 591. https://doi.org/10.7326/m15-2239.

Watson, K., & Fu, B. (2016). Medical Improv: A novel approach to teaching communication and professionalism skills. Annals of Internal Medicine, 165(8), 591-592. https://doi.org/10.7326/m15-2239.

Watson, K. & Fu, B. (2020). What is Medical Improv? https://www.medicalimprov.org/about.

Weberg, D. (2012). Complexity Leadership: A Healthcare Imperative. Nursing Forum, 47(4),

268–277. https://doi.org/10.1111/j.1744-6198.2012.00276.x.

West, M.A. (1996). Reflexivity and work group effectiveness: A conceptual integration.

West, M. A. (2021). Compassionate leadership: sustaining wisdom, humanity and presence in health and social care. Swirling Leaf Press.

West, M., Bailey, S., & Williams, E. (2020). The courage of compassion. Supporting Nurses and Midwives to Deliver High-Quality Care, London: The King's Fund, London.

West, M. A., Borrill, C. S., Dawson, J. F., Brodbeck, F., Shapiro, D. A., & Haward, B. (2003). Leadership clarity and team innovation in health care. The Leadership Quarterly, 14(4–5), 393–410. https://doi.org/10.1016/s1048-9843(03)00044-4.

West, M., & Coia, D. (2019). Caring for doctors, caring for patients. General Medical Council. https://www.rcpe.ac.uk/sites/default/files/caring_for_doctors.pdf

Williamson, O. E. (1985). The economic institutions of capitalism. New York: Free Press.

Willumsen, E. (2016). Tverrprofesjonelt samarbeid i utdanning og praksis i helse- og velferdssektoren. In E. Willumsen & A. Ødegård (Eds.),Tverrprofesjonelt samarbeid : Et samfunnsoppdrag (2 ed., pp. 33–52).Universitetsforlaget.

Withey, M. J., & Cooper, W. H. (1989). Predicting exit, voice, loyalty, and neglect. Administrative Science Quarterly, 34(4), 521. https://doi.org/10.2307/2393565.

Woo, C. H., & Lee, M. J. (2018). The effect of hospital organizational culture, organizational silence and job embeddedness on turnover intention of general hospital nurses. Journal of Digital Convergence, 16(3), 385-394. https://doi.org/10.14400/JDC.2018.16.3.385.

World Health Organization. (2010). Framework for action on interprofessional education and collaborative practice. https://www.who.int/publications/i/item/framework-for-action-on-interprofessional-education-collaborative-practice.

Wu, M., Li, W., Zhang, L., Zhang, C., & Zhou, H. (2023). Workplace suspicion, knowledge hiding, and silence behavior: A double-moderated mediation model of knowledge-based psychological ownership and face consciousness. Frontiers in Psychology, 14, 982440. https://doi.org/10.3389/fpsyg.2023.982440.

Xu, A. J., Loi, R., and Lam, L. W. (2015). The bad boss takes it all: How abusive supervision and leader–member exchange interact to influence employee silence. The Leadership Quarterly, 26(5), 763–774. https://doi.org/10.1016/j.leaqua.2015.03.002.

Yağar, F., & Dumke Yağar, S. (2023). The effects of organizational silence on work engagement, intention to leave and job performance levels of nurses. Work, 75(2), 471-478. https://doi.org/0.3233/WOR-210192.

Yurdakul, M., Beşen, M. A., & Erdoğan, S. (2016). The organisational silence of midwives and nurses: reasons and results. Journal of Nursing Management, 24(5), 686–694. https://doi.org/10.1111/jonm.12374.

Zheng, Y. H. E., Palombella, A., Salfi, J., & Wainman, B. (2019). Dissecting through barriers: A follow-up study on the long-term effects of interprofessional education in a dissection course with healthcare professional students. Anatomical Sciences Education, 12 (1), 52–60. https://doi.org/10.1002/ase.1791.

Appendix A

Role-Playing Activities Template
Kolb's Experiential Learning Perspective

Scenario Title:

Participants:

Setting:

Communication Issue:

Concrete Experience (Feeling — Describe what happened)

Reflective Observation (Watching — Think and reflect on what happened)

Abstract Conceptualization (Analyze)

What happened?

What went wrong?

What should be done next time to prevent miscommunication?

How could communication be improved within the team?

Active Experimentation (Practice what you have learned)

What would you do the next time something similar happens?

How do you feel after this analysis process?

Was the analysis productive?

How will this experience impact your future decisions as a communicator?

Presenting the Author

The author of the book *Communication Among Healthcare Professionals* has extensive experience in the field as a clinical physical therapist for almost forty years. Driven by her love for the profession, she started to teach ten years ago. Her experience ranges from providing clinical service to her patients, teaching and clinical advising to health and academic entities, to collaborating in accreditation processes for institutes, universities, and healthcare corporations. Communication is essential for effective performance in these settings.

Dr. Berríos is known by her colleagues and students as a kind person who is open to dialogue and enjoys teamwork. Readers of this text will appreciate the analysis of real case studies, full of wisdom and practical knowledge, leading to the development of understanding and collaboration. They will navigate through situations similar to those found in their workplaces or academic institutions. She offers tools to identify factors and barriers that affect communication, allowing us to learn about causes and solutions. Speaking, remaining silent, or modulating our voices are different ways of making ourselves understood. Developing psychological safety, trust, and collaboration is hard to achieve but attainable. Effective communication will facilitate conflict resolution.

I have known and shared a lifelong friendship and worked professionally with the author for over four decades. I am positive that you will enjoy the book and use every recommendation Dr. Berrios offers.

Thank you, Dr. Berríos, for the honor of presenting you to your readers.

Roberto Vélez Santiago, BA, MA, MEd, EdD

Dr. Iris Mercedes Berríos Rivera studied physical therapy at the University of Puerto Rico School of Health Professions. Years later, she completed a master's in public health, becoming a specialist in mother and child health at Universidad de Puerto Rico Recinto de Ciencias Médicas. Then, she completed a transitional Doctor in Physical Therapy degree in 2017 at the University of St. Augustine for Health Sciences, where she also completed a Doctor in Education degree in 2024.

For correspondence: irismercedesberrios2024@gmail.com